Hooked On Minnesota

Best wishes...
[signature]
11/10/08

Hooked On Minnesota

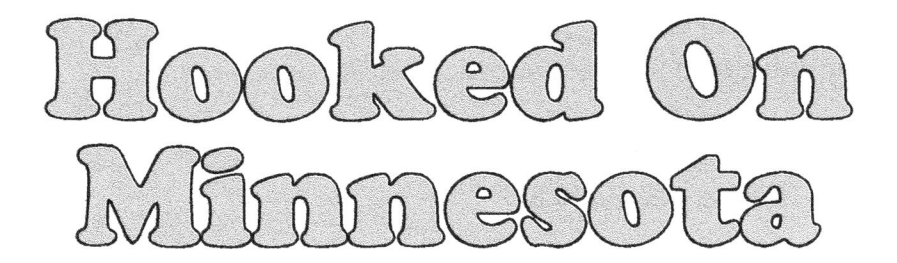

Guide to the Good Life

by Dick Hill

Beaver's Pond Press, Inc.

Edina, Minnesota

HOOKED ON MINNESOTA © copyright 2008 by Dick Hill. All rights reserved. No part of this book may be reproduced in any form whatsoever, by photography or xerography or by any other means, by broadcast or transmission, by translation into any kind of language, nor by recording electronically or otherwise, without permission in writing from the author, except by a reviewer, who may quote brief passages in critical articles or reviews.

ISBN 10: 1-59298-260-3
ISBN 13: 978-1-59298-260-8

Library of Congress Control Number: 2008939184
Printed in the United States of America
First Printing: October 2008
12 11 10 09 08   6 5 4 3 2 1

Cover and interior design by Clay Schotzko

Beaver's Pond Press, Inc.

Beaver's Pond Press is an imprint of
Beaver's Pond Group
7104 Ohms Lane
Edina, MN 55439-2129
(952) 829-8818
www.BeaversPondPress.com

Dedication

*To everyone who has
a Minnesota connection.
And for those who moved away,
may* Hooked On Minnesota
take you home again.

Contents

Preface xi

Foreword xiii

About the Author xvi

Acknowledgements xvii

Chapter One: Great Place to Live 1
   Our Good Life 1
   Pines, Mines & Lakes 4
   Why I Love Minnesota 9

Chapter Two: Vacationland 11
   Land of 10,000 Lakes 11
   Resort Vacations 14
   Top Ten Lakes 18
   Voyageurs National Park 23
   Lake Kabetogama 27
   The Boundary Waters (BWCA) 30
   Itasca State Park 35
   State Record Fish 37
   Top Ten Campgrounds 38
   Duluth's Lake Superior 40
   Mr. North Woods' Hot Spots 43
   Ten Favorite Bait Shops 47
   Top Ten Metro Parks 49

Chapter Three: Dining & Places to Go 50
    MOA (Mall of America) 50
    Hidden Treasures...................................... 53
    Judy Garland Museum 56
    Top Ten Restaurants 60
    Best Shopping.. 64
    Favorite Places 66
    Sarah Jane's Bakery 67
    Curious Side Trips 69

Chapter Four: Four Seasons of Fun 73
    Festivals & Events 73
    Winter Wonderland................................... 77
    Minnetonka's Icy Plunge 80
    Minnesota Picnics 81
    Nature and Vacation Photo Tips 82
    County Fairs.. 87
    Minnesota State Fair 92
    Minnesota Casinos.................................... 96

Chapter Five: Minnesota Legends 98
    Weather Watch 98
    WCCO 8-3-0 Radio 99
    Minnesota Mile Markers............................. 103
    Best Books 106
    Minnesota Celebrities 110
    All Star Team 116
    Paul Bunyan and Pals 120

Chapter Six: Business Minded 124
    Minnesota Made 124

Chapter Seven: Minnesota Memories 127
   Nostalgic Notables. 127
   Soda Fountains. 131
   Movies—A Mini Vacation. 133

Chapter Eight: Prize Catches 136
   Trivia Answers 136
   Minnesota Nice 139

Preface

Minnesota is special. I know. I have tried other places. But I am much wiser now. I realize life is too short to live anywhere else. Minnesota is a great place to live, work, and raise a family. My wife, Mary, agrees. She says that she needs her Byerly's "grocery fix" at least once a week.

Minnesota is one of the nation's top livable places. National research and surveys praise our K–12 public school systems. We also shine in higher learning. And our hospitals and health clinics are rated among the best in America.

We are headquarters for 20 *Fortune* 500 companies. Our strong corporate base offers a diverse workplace.

Minnesota offers some of the most productive family farms to be found anywhere, all contributing to our important agribusiness.

The Twin Cities of Minneapolis and St. Paul have the most vibrant performing arts community. If you are drawn to the arts, you can indulge yourself with Minnesota's offerings—art museums, symphony and jazz concerts, dance, opera, musicals, and Broadway touring shows.

If it is fun you are after, we rank seventh in the top ten of the "most fun" states. In the four seasons of Minnesota, there is a $10 billion annual tourism industry featuring 900 resorts, 500 campgrounds, 72 state parks, 58 state forests, one national park, two national monuments, one national wilderness area, 16 national wildlife refuge areas, 22 scenic byways, including six with national designations, covering almost 2,800 miles, 500 golf courses, 800 annual festivals, 18 casinos, and renowned shopping spots, including one megamall!

What I am leading up to is a selection of Minnesota's great wonders, many natural, others manmade, and many featured in this book.

Minnesota's Top Ten Wonders

1. 10,000 lakes, including one Great—Lake Superior (Gateway to the World)
2. MOA (Mall of America), Bloomington
3. The Boundary Waters Canoe Area (BWCA), Superior National Forest
4. The Mayo Clinic (World's Health Clinic), Rochester
5. University of Minnesota (Leader in Education), Twin Cities, Duluth, Crookston, and Morris
6. Minnesota State Fair (The Great Get-Together), St. Paul
7. Mississippi Headwaters
8. Paul Bunyan in Akeley, Bemidji, Brainerd, and Chisholm
9. Minnesota Casinos, located in 19 cities, including Prior Lake, Hinkley, Grand Portage, and Morton
10. Voyageurs National Park, International Falls

Hooked on Minnesota is your guide to Minnesota's good life. You will find dozens of places to go, shop, dine, picnic, swim, fish, sightsee, and vacation. After reading the tales, trivia, and facts in the book, I believe you will be as hooked on Minnesota as I am.

Foreword

By Dana Pitt
President, Congress of Minnesota Resorts

I love Minnesota and its tourism heritage, and I leap at the chance to tell people about it. Minnesota has a history rich in family resorts, and I have been part of that for a good portion of my life. I own and operate Bailey's Resort, together with my wife, Cindy, on the west end of Leech Lake near Walker. We are beginning our tenth season. We enjoy being part of our guests' vacation tradition at the lake. Many folks have been coming to Bailey's for generations and are not only our guests, but also our friends. We are proud to be members of the Congress of Minnesota Resorts. One year we received "Resorters of the Year" recognition. This is my first time as its president.

The Congress of Minnesota Resorts is a unique association, dedicated to helping visitors experience an enjoyable and memorable vacation in our state. "Resorters" have been an essential part of Minnesota Tourism for nearly one hundred years. Our motto says it all: "Resorters Helping Resorters." The esprit de corps among us is genuine. We exchange ideas to help each other have greater success. We also work closely with Explore Minnesota Tourism, the Department of Natural Resources (DNR), the state legislature, the governor, and other organizations. Every year, our members appear en masse at the state capitol in St. Paul to help support tourism. We try to make a big splash, so one year we all wore bright orange lifejackets, and once we carried giant bobber coolers during our "day on the hill." We are an enthusiastic group and are always easy to spot among the legislators. Maybe you have read about us, or seen us on TV.

People are amazed when I tell them we are part of a $10 billion industry. But that is how valuable and important tourism is to Minnesota.

The choices for resort vacations are many, from large complexes with luxury suites, on-site golf courses, spas, and gourmet restaurants to rustic lodges with the charm and quiet solitude that only a smaller resort can provide. Many resorts are open year round for Minnesota's four seasons of fun. And although fishing remains a focal point, resorts today offer so much more, as Dick Hill's book highlights such as boating, swimming, hiking, biking, sightseeing, relaxing, taking in local community events, meeting new friends, and spending quality family time. Hill has done a wonderful job capturing the aspects of Minnesota that make this state so special in *Hooked on Minnesota*. The book showcases Minnesota's great wonders—from the bustling Mall of America to the untouched wilderness—showing that "Land of 10,000 Lakes" has something for everyone, visitors and residents alike. As my wife, Cindy, observed, *Hooked on Minnesota* is the next best thing to a Minnesota vacation. Enjoy!

About Dana Pitt

Dana Pitt is a lifelong Minnesotan. He loves the north woods lifestyle and the resort business. He, his wife Cindy, and their children, Drew, Jake, and Rachel, live on Kabekona Bay in the Chippewa National Forest. The Pitts own the nine-cabin Bailey's Resort on Leech Lake. Their children, aged 6–12, may become the next generation of great "resorters." Dana is serving as president of the Congress of Minnesota Resorts; he also serves on the Board of Directors for both the Leech Lake Area Chamber of Commerce and the Leech Lake Tourism Bureau and is a member of the Leech Lake Fishing Task Force.

Cindy and Dana Pitt, owners of Bailey's Resort on Leech Lake, Walker, with children (l to r): Drew, 12, Rachel, 6, and Jake, 10. Dana is serving as president of the Congress of Minnesota Resorts. (Photo courtesy Bailey's Resort)

About the Author

Minnesota-born Dick Hill is a five-star author who has earned numerous creative, marketing, and broadcasting awards. His books include *Battle Talk!* (Five Star Winner) and *Advertising That Sells*, a handbook for the State of Minnesota's Small Business Centers. Hill, a graduate of the University of Minnesota, survived a 35-year advertising career including 12 years with Campbell Mithun. He is president of Dick Hill Advertising and lives with his wife, Mary, in Edina, Minnesota. Their car's license plate reads *HKDONMN*, acronym for the title of this book.

Acknowledgements

A special "Thank you" to everyone involved. Including the following:

- Congress of Minnesota Resorts
- Minnesota Historical Society
- Explore Minnesota Tourism
- Mall of America
- Minnesota State Fair
- Judy Garland Museum
- Visit Bemidji
- Candy Jackson
- Alan Burchell

Chapter One
Great Place to Live

Our Good Life
Minnesota is a special place to live, learn, and work

> Even though we were drained from working hard, we still had the energy for the fun things: swimming, fishing, hunting, hiking, and camping. Minnesota was an ideal environment while growing up. The lakes, creeks, ponds, woods, and trails were right at our front door.
>
> Excerpt from Remembering Rosy
> Esther Johnson Connell, Itasca County

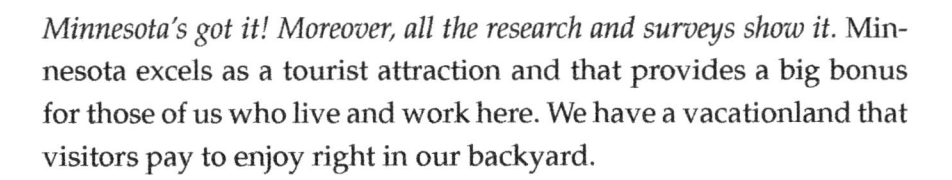

Minnesota's got it! Moreover, all the research and surveys show it. Minnesota excels as a tourist attraction and that provides a big bonus for those of us who live and work here. We have a vacationland that visitors pay to enjoy right in our backyard.

Residents love Minnesota because it does indeed offer an enriched lifestyle. There are north woods, prairies, bluffs, rivers, and cityscapes to enjoy and explore. All you have to do is look around.

The cultural community in the Twin Cities of Minneapolis and St. Paul includes; the Minnesota Orchestra, The Saint Paul Chamber Orchestra, Ordway Center for the Performing Arts, The Children's

Canoeing Lake Bemidji. (Photo courtesy Larry Young)

Theatre Company, Penumbra Theater Company, Old Log Theater, Chanhassen Dinner Theater, the Hennepin Theatre District, Theatre de la Jeune Lune, the Guthrie Theater, the Minnesota Centennial Showboat, Minneapolis Institute of Arts, Walker Art Center, and the Frederick R. Weisman Art Museum. And families enjoy the Minnesota Children's Museum, Science Museum of Minnesota, the Minnesota History Center, the Minnesota Zoo, the Marjorie McNeely Conservatory, and the Minnesota Landscape Arboretum.

Our sports venue is rich in tradition. We have the Minnesota Twins, who have two World Series victories, the Minnesota Vikings, the Minnesota Timberwolves, the Minnesota Lynx, the Minnesota Thunder and the Minnesota Wild. Plus there is the collegiate Golden Gophers' full sports program. No one can match our High School Hockey Tournament that thousands live for each March, including Lou Nanne, the coach of the former Minnesota North Stars professional hockey team.

Up north, where Paul Bunyan lives, the good life is in the fishing, hunting, boating, swimming, state parks, and campgrounds. And for the entire package, there are hundreds of resorts that provide accommodations and wonderful Minnesota vacation memories.

The southern Minnesota prairies and river bluffs offer varying scenic vistas from blooming wildflowers to restful valleys. Amish buggies may appear on the winding roads. There are great bike trails along the Root River and Harmony-Preston Valley. You can visit resident artists' studios and galleries or stay at a cozy bed-and-breakfast inn.

In addition to all of the above, Minnesota is a good place for employment. Our Blue Chip companies, such as 3M, General Mills (called one of the top employers in the nation), Hormel, Mayo Clinic, SuperValu, and our ever growing health care industry—offer viable workplaces for Minnesotans. And there is the Target Corporation, Best Buy, Lunds & Byerly's, shopping centers at the Mall of America, Southdale, Ridgedale, Roseville, Burnsville, Maplewood, Eden Prairie, the Galleria, and thousands of retail outlets.

We saved the best for last: education. Living here, we may be too close to the forest to see the trees. However, many outsiders know. They come to our state to take advantage of the best in high schools, the University of Minnesota (founded in 1851), and our many technical schools and colleges. There are 17 four-year liberal-arts colleges with world-class reputations, such as St. Olaf and Gustavus Adolphus. In addition, two of our technical schools, Dunwoody Institute and Brown College, have been around for more than 60 years. They successfully train and graduate thousands of students. Minnesota is also the proud home of MacPhail Center for Music, which just celebrated its centennial year. MacPhail transforms lives and enriches our community through music education and performances.

It is perfectly clear. Minnesota, with its opportunities, good life and invaluable resources, including our 10,000 lakes, is a great place to live, learn, and visit.

Pines, Mines, and Lakes
What we are all about; Our Minnesota profile

Minnesota became a territory in 1849 and the Thirty-second state in 1858. The name "Minnesota" comes from Dakota Indian words meaning "water that reflects the sky," or, as more-often translated "sky-blue waters."

"Make no small plans, for no one will remember them." It is obvious that our first state governor, Henry Sibley, in 1858, followed this advice and had big plans for our state. He recognized the state's vast wealth of natural resources, especially Minnesota's extensive timberlands and fertile prairie that were the basis for Minnesota's early industrial development. His vision helped give Minnesota a solid foundation for growth. In the late nineteenth century, Minneapolis was the nation's flour-milling center. By the early twentieth century, canning and meatpacking were among the state's largest industries.

Henry Sibley was influential in using "Minnesota" vs. "Itasca," the name preferred by the territorial bill's sponsor, Stephen A. Douglas. That is a good thing, because "sky-blue waters" gave us one of the most recognized themes in America: *The Land of 10,000 Lakes.*

View of Lake Itasca from Douglas Lodge.
(Photo courtesy Minnesota Historical Society)

Minnesota's 150 Years of Statehood (1858–2008) is something to celebrate. And the sky is the limit for the future.

Industries: Agriculture, manufacturing, forestry, tourism, mining, printing, publishing, and health care.

Capital: St. Paul

Population:
State of Minnesota: 5,132,799
Minneapolis: 387,711
St. Paul: (Capital) 287,385
Rochester: 90,515
Duluth: 85,889
Bloomington: 84,347

Number of counties: 87

State symbols:
Flower: Showy Lady's slipper
Bird: Loon
Fish: Walleye
Tree: Red Norway pine
Song: "Hail Minnesota"
Fruit: Honeycrisp Apple
Drink: Milk
Grain: Wild Rice
Butterfly: Monarch
Gemstone: Lake Superior Agate

Minnesota's State Seal. (Author's collection)

Legends:
Paul Bunyan

Hiawatha
Minnehaha

Nicknames:
Land of 10,000 Lakes
Gopher State
North Star State

Geography:
Length: Slightly over 400 miles
Width: 200–350 miles
Land area: 83,574 square miles
Water area: 7,326 square miles
Total area: 90,900 square miles (12th largest of the 50 states)
Mean Elevation: 1,200 feet above sea level
Highest point: 2,301 feet at Eagle Mountain
Lowest point: 602 feet at Lake Superior shore
Location: Upper Midwest, North Central United States. Minnesota is bordered by Canada on the north, Iowa on the south, Lake Superior and Wisconsin on the east, and North and South Dakota on the west.

Minnesota waters:
Major rivers: Minnesota, Mississippi, Rainy, Red of the North, and St. Croix
11,871 lakes (more than 10 acres)
69,200 miles of rivers and streams
Minnesota borders Lake Superior, which is the world's largest freshwater lake. It is the furthest west of the five Great Lakes at the end of the St. Lawrence Seaway, which brings ships from around the world to the Port of Duluth.

Weather:
Average annual snowfall: 53–70 inches
Normal annual precipitation: 19–34 inches
Twin Cities average temperatures:

	High/Low
January 31	21°F/1°F
April 30	62°F/41°F
July 31	83°F/60°F
September 30	65°F/42°F

Colloquialisms:
Uff da!
You betcha!
Yeah!
Minnesota nice
Lutefisk

Minnesota's Commemorative Quarter, a collector's item, one of the 50 State Quarters. (Photo courtesy The United States Mint)

Why I Love Minnesota
By Roger Erickson, former WCCO Radio announcer

> A fan of WCCO Radio for many years, I enjoyed all the great announcers, including Cedric Adams and Clellan Card. After those two legends left the airwaves, two new fellows eventually came along—Charlie Boone and Roger Erickson. They were one of the best teams in broadcasting. They had a special knack when doing interviews. In addition, all of the big-name celebrities and politicians seemed to be accessible to them. They were skilled in writing, telling stories, and, of course, acting. Roger Erickson worked at WCCO radio for 39 years. He also starred for three years as the beloved children's character "Bozo the Clown" on WCCO-TV. He is a 2001 Charter Inductee in the Museum of Broadcasting Hall of Fame.
>
> *—Author's highlights*

I love Minnesota because of its four distinct seasons. And please don't laugh, but my favorite months are May and October. I even like January—I think.

I love all sports—and that includes the University of Minnesota's teams. The Golden Gophers were our major league long before the professional teams arrived in the state. The university's basketball and football teams still thrill me to this day, as does the Minnesota Marching Band . . . such precision.

I love all the theater—professional and amateur. (I had better say that, as I met my wife while performing in a play, although I did not like the fact that she got more applause than I did.) Overall, the arts scene is wonderful here.

I am sure that I join all Minnesotans and visitors who are thrilled every time they experience the lakes and woods of our great northland. I was so captivated myself that I took a geology course at the University of Minnesota to find out how it all happened.

Now, having said all that, I have to tell you that I am a child of the prairie. Every time I visit my hometown of Winthrop, I spend time just looking at the land—that endless stretch of rich black soil—interrupted only by the farmsteads nestled in those protective groves of trees. And as you look way off in the distance, those groves get smaller and smaller—until they are specs. Oh, one more thing. You may have seen a sunset over some ocean, but wait until you have seen one on the Minnesota prairie.

CRAGUN'S
Resort and Hotel on Gull Lake

Chapter Two
Vacationland

Land of 10,000 Lakes
Our sky blue waters attract visitors

> As a kid from Detroit, I was sure impressed with the world of activities that Minnesota had to offer during my summer vacations. It was easy for me to understand why my great-great-grandparents had moved from their Irish homestead to settle their family in Grand Rapids, near the headwaters of the Mississippi. I enjoyed camping out the most. I will never forget the hidden jewel lakes nestled in the northern pine forests. I intend to continue this tradition by taking my wife, Jurgita, and two sons to the same trophy fishing lakes that my uncle Ray Connell introduced me to as a child.
>
> —Robert John Strimpel, General Motors
> Mexico City, Mexico

"COME TO MINNESOTA," was one of the earliest headlines for our state's tourism efforts in 1917. And it worked. It was the idea of The Ten Thousand Lakes of Minnesota Association, a group of 50 communities, our first pioneers in tourism. The resort owners wanted to fill their cabins, the merchants, their stores. They raised $50,000 to attract visitors to Minnesota's natural wonders. It would be $500,000 in 2008 dollars. The association placed advertisements nationwide, funded a movie about canoeing on the Mississippi

*Canoeing on the Boundary Waters, one of Minnesota's great wonders.
(Photo courtesy Explore Minnesota Tourism)*

River, and published a range of beautifully illustrated pamphlets and postcards touting Minnesota's obvious and varied vacation opportunities. Moreover, they did it all on their own. No help from the state—or even an advertising agency. Smartly, they first counted Minnesota's lakes. Ten thousand seemed like a good number to promote. (Actually, Minnesota has 11,871, but our state is known for understating the facts.) Our state parks, with their majestic forests, also helped build our tourism industry. Plus, we had the cabins, resorts, outfitters and campgrounds to accommodate the visitors. Thus, we became a nationally recognized vacationland.

The "Land of 10,000 Lakes" theme was a stroke of marketing genius. It is burned in the minds of most Americans—even stamped on our license plates. That is how most people in other states picture us. The Ten Thousand Lakes of Minnesota Association turned the tourism efforts over to Minnesota's Bureau of Tourism in the Department of Conservation in the 1930s. Today, the state's tourism promotion branch, Explore Minnesota Tourism, reports that the industry brings $10 billion into Minnesota annually. Nice return on investment from that $50,000 seed money used to attract visitors to the Land of 10,000 Lakes.

Lake City takes credit for the nation's first water skiing. Ralph Samuelson, 18 years old, came up with the idea on beautiful Lake Pepin. His invention in 1922 launched a new summer sport and industry.

Resort Vacations
Making Minnesota Vacation Memories

> *Fishing and hunting were my greatest pleasures growing up in Minnesota. My wife, Marj, and I still try to visit the northern area (Grand Rapids) every year or so, and I inevitably end up on a dock with my fishing pole in hand. One morning I was casting my line into the Mississippi by the Blandin Paper Mill, having no luck, when I noticed another "fisherman"—an awesome American bald eagle. He was fishing for his breakfast, swooping majestically overhead, his "eagle eye" trained on the placid waters. Suddenly he dove and connected with his target. I waited expectantly for him to fly away, triumphant and intent on breakfast. That did not happen. He flapped, shifted, and strained to take off but obviously, he had bitten off more than he could chew, so to speak. Not willing to give up his plan, he flapped his sturdy wings and proceeded to "row" his catch to shore. It took him several minutes before he pulled the large fish to the sandy shore and stood triumphantly atop his fishing trophy. Within a few minutes, his mate had joined him, and they took turns feasting on the morning's catch. [There is] so much beauty and bounty in Minnesota.*
>
> —Bob Connell
> Anaheim, California

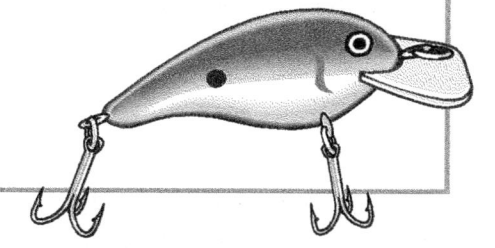

Minnesota's hundreds of resorts, lodges, and outfitters offer the ideal stay for most anyone. And the choices are wide, from large complexes with luxury suites, on-site golf courses, spas, and gourmet restaurants to rustic historic lodges providing large quantities of charm and fun. Many are open during the winter to accommodate those pursuing cross-country skiing, ice fishing, and snowmobiling. Like the earliest settlers, Minnesota resort owners (called resorters) are a hearty bunch and pioneers in promoting resort vacations. Today, hundreds of them have banded together to make sure visitors enjoy their Minnesota resort vacations to the fullest.

The Congress of Minnesota Resorts is their industry association dedicated to the mission of helping family-owned and operated resorts in Minnesota to continue as a viable segment of the Minnesota Tourism Industry. Teamwork-minded, its slogan is "Resorters Helping Resorters." Their shared expertise ultimately helps visitors enjoy their vacations to the fullest. Resorters want visitors to enjoy their stays and bring home memorable experiences. In addition, the association makes it easy for visitors to find the right resort for their needs. You can visit their website, www.minnesota-resorts.com, for more information. After you settle in at the resort, you can count on your hosts to suggest fun activities—and to provide answers to your many questions:

- What is the best time for fishing?
- Where is the top spot for catching the big ones?
- What kind are they catching?
- Do you use any special hook or bait?
- How deep is the lake?
- What is my limit?
- Is there golf in the area?
- What festivals or events are going on?
- Can we book space now for next year?

Their theme, "Resorters Helping Resorters," is the driving force behind this association. (Photo courtesy Congress of Minnesota Resorts)

To help you get started in your search for the right resort, here are several to consider:

- Geneva Beach Resort, Alexandria
- Tepee-Tonka Resort, Blackduck
- Cragun's Resort on Gull Lake, Brainerd
- Madden's Resort on Gull Lake, Brainerd
- Grand View Lodge, Gull Lake, Brainerd
- Breezy Point Resort, Breezy Point
- Moose Lake Resort, Deer River
- Ruttgers Bay Lake Lodge, Deerwood
- Wilderness Bay Lodge, Ely
- Pine Acres Resort, Grand Rapids
- Gunflint Lodge, on the Gunflint Trail, Grand Marais
- Bert's Cabins, Lake Itasca
- Moosehorn Resort, Lake Kabetogema
- Bailey's Resort on Leech Lake, Walker
- Shing Wako Resort, Merrifield
- Cedar Rapids Lodge, Tenstrike

The American bald eagle, the nation's emblem, is a majestic and common sight in northern Minnesota. (Photo courtesy Alan Burchell)

Happy guest fishing off the dock at Moosehorn Resort, Kabetogama, while waiting for the rest of his group to come to the boat. (Photo courtesy Alan Burchell)

Top Ten Lakes
Not easy, picking ten out of 10,000

My Minnesota memories helped me survive the seven years I was a POW in a Vietnam prison camp. Day after day, I recalled my youth living at 2730 Elliott Avenue South, Minneapolis close to the Sears Lake Street store. Our family was blessed: three girls and boys. We attended Holy Rosary Catholic Church. Had we lived across the alley, I could have gone to St. Stephen's with my good buddy, Charlie Parker. We played baseball and skated at Stewart Field, across from Greeley, my first school. We would spend summer nights at band concerts at Powderhorn Park and buy buttered popcorn from one of the two horse-drawn popcorn wagons. We went everywhere with our bikes. Some of my best memories were of Lake Calhoun when I worked the canoe concession. Like most kids, we would swipe apples on the way back home. I got pretty good at remembering the little things in my life. The guards at our POW camp would try to "break us," but they couldn't touch our memories.

—Richard E. Bolstad
Englewood, Florida

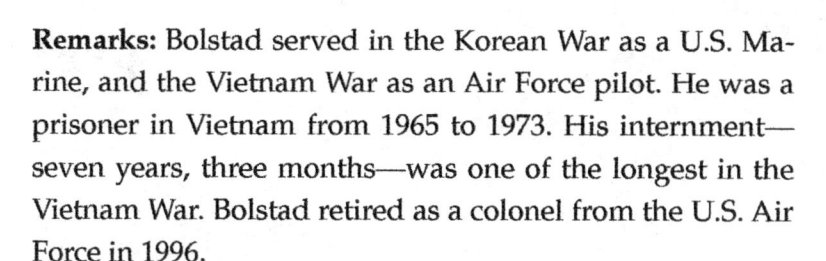

Remarks: Bolstad served in the Korean War as a U.S. Marine, and the Vietnam War as an Air Force pilot. He was a prisoner in Vietnam from 1965 to 1973. His internment—seven years, three months—was one of the longest in the Vietnam War. Bolstad retired as a colonel from the U.S. Air Force in 1996.

Minneapolis native, Dick Bolstad, and wife, Sissy. (Photo courtesy Dick Bolstad)

Minnesota is modest. There actually are 11,871 lakes in our state. (They have to be 10 acres or more to qualify.) Bring a digital camera. You will want to record the beauty of these lakes:

1. **Lake Mille Lacs**, Garrison. This is one of the top fishing lakes specializing in walleye, northern pike, rock bass, muskie and bluegill. Small and large bass and sunnies are also caught. With more than 75 miles of shoreline, it is Minnesota's second-largest lake. Maximum depth is only 42 feet. It has plenty of resorts, camping spots, and bait shops.

The winter brings a city of icehouses to the lake. Many celebrities have fished there, including football broadcaster John Madden, who went ice fishing on a dare in 1983 while covering a Vikings football game.

2. **Lake Pokegama**, Grand Rapids. Ideal for fishing, swimming, and boating, Lake Pokegama is easily accessible by using any of four boat landings. Pokegama is a good fishing ground for walleye and small mouth bass, plus lots of panfish. The community puts on a superb Fourth of July fireworks display too good to miss. It is just minutes from shopping and downtown Grand Rapids.

3. **Lake Winnibigoshish**, north of Deer River. Lake Winnie is popular with walleye and musky anglers. The state record musky (54 pounds; 56 inches long) was caught there in 1957. Seems like the farther north the bigger the fish. Much of the land around Winnie is part of the Chippewa National Forest. The area is great to picnic.

4. **Lake of the Woods**, Baudette. Welcome to the walleye capital of the world. And be sure to get a picture with Willie Walleye, the giant icon at Baudette. The area provides a vacation of a lifetime including a winter wonderland of cross-country skiing, snowmobiling, and ice fishing.

An angler paradise, Minnesota offers over 90,000 miles of shoreline—more than California, Florida, and Hawaii combined.

5. **Lake Superior**, Duluth. Superior is the largest of the five Great Lakes, and an important link in the Great Lakes Waterway. You can fish for lake trout, brown trout, salmon, walleye, bass, and smelt. It is also a great vacation kick-off spot. The picturesque North Shore has eight state parks. Farther north along Highway 61 is Split Rock Lighthouse overlooking Lake Superior. The Minnesota Historical Society operates it, and it is on the National Register of Historic Places.
6. **Lake Minnetonka**, Excelsior. With 140 miles of shoreline, Lake Minnetonka is really a series of small lakes connected by short canals. The best fishing is for largemouth and smallmouth bass. A great lake for sailing, although there are many speedboaters too. The area is steeped in history. A good place to start your journey is at the Lake Minnetonka Gift Shop. You will find posters and books about Excelsior, Wayzata, Minnetonka, the bays, and more. Besides the fishing, there are cruises, Old Log Theater (in Excelsior, south of the lake), dozens of restaurants with boat docks and souvenir spots. It is located just minutes west of the Twin Cities. Every New Year's Day, there is an icy plunge event at the Bay View Event Center in Excelsior.
7. **Lake Calhoun**, Minneapolis. Lake Calhoun has three beaches for swimmers, plus fishing, sailing, windsurfing, kayaking, canoeing, paddleboats, and electric fun boats, not to mention walking, roller and in-line skating, and bicycle trails that encircle the lake and connect to the city's chain-of-lakes and Minnehaha Creek trail system. Lake Calhoun features "The Milk Carton Boat Races" during the summer Aquatennial. In the winter, it becomes icehouse country.

The nearby Lake Street area offers a ton of shopping and eating places.

8. **Lake of the Isles**, Minneapolis. Linked to Calhoun by a channel for non-motorized boats is the beautiful Lake of the Isles, offering a park-like atmosphere. Take a three-mile hike or bike ride around the lake. Canoeing is popular, as is ice skating in the winter. Many people prefer to bring a blanket and relax with a book or people watching.

9. **White Bear Lake**, White Bear Lake. A northeastern suburb just 20 minutes from Minneapolis/St. Paul is White Bear Lake, named for an Ojibwe legend about a white bear. Covering 10 square miles, it offers residents and visitors good pan fishing, boating, sailing, and swimming. Pontoon and boat rentals are available. In January, take in the St. Paul Winter Carnival Event, Bear'ly Open Golf Tournament on Ice on White Bear Lake.

10. **Bush Lake**, Bloomington. Here is a hidden jewel in the middle of metro suburban Minneapolis. It is part of the Hyland-Bush-Anderson Lakes Regional Park, just south of Interstate Highway 494 on Bush Lake Road. Pack a picnic, fishing gear, and your swimming suit to enjoy the full benefit of Bush Lake. Nice fishing piers help you pull in those big ones.

MOA has more annual visitors than the combined populations of Iowa, North Dakota, South Dakota, and Canada. See you there.

Voyageurs National Park
Visitors awed by its majestic beauty

> The uniquely scenic and historic Voyageurs National Park stands as a monument forever to the dedicated citizens and conservation organizations whose vision, ingenuity, and courage match the splendor of this superlative wilderness area. Rich in the history of the early, exciting exploration of our great country, Voyageurs will serve as a living legacy linking generation to generation and century to century.
>
> —*Voyageurs National Park Act*
> *January 8, 1971*

Voyageurs National Park near International Falls in northeastern St. Louis County is the most incredible 218,000-acre water-based park you may ever experience. The interconnected scenic waterways offer plenty of year-round opportunities for exploration, recreation, fishing, swimming, camping, and wildlife watching. The memory of Voyageurs National Park—the sky blue waters, wildflowers, and untouched wilderness—is unforgettable.

Voyageurs National Park has no roads, except for winter ice ones, so most visitors enter by water. The park consists of Rainy (60 miles long), Kabetogama (15 miles long), Namakan (16 miles long), and Sandpoint (8 miles long) lakes as well as 30 small inland lakes and some 900 islands. The waterways flow west into the Rainy River between Minnesota and Ontario, Canada, and then north into Hudson Bay. Kabetogama Peninsula includes the park's largest land-

Boat buddies at Voyageurs National Park. (Photo courtesy Alan Burchell)

mass, which is only accessible by water during the warmer months or by crossing the frozen ice in the winter.

Public launch ramps are available along with visitor centers on Rainy Lake on the shore of Black Bay (open year round, 888-381-2873), Kabetogama Lake (open May–September, 218-875-2111) and Ash River (open May–September, 218-374-3221). Numerous resorts also offer boat access into the park. Boat tours and naturalist programs offered in the summer.

Visitors can explore Voyageurs National Park by motorized boat, rowboat, canoe, kayak, or houseboat. And unlike the Boundary Waters (BWCA), there is no restriction on using motorized boats. There are over 200 campsites available by boat only. You can hike on 45 miles of designated trails with either water or land access and in the winter cross country ski or snowshoe. There are also 110 miles of marked and groomed snowmobile trails in the park. The International Voyageurs Snowmobile Club maintains 134 miles of groomed trails in the area around the park.

Bring your camera, as Voyageurs is home to a rich variety wilderness and wildlife: there are 42 mammals including wolf, black bear, moose, fox, and deer; 240 birds including bald eagle, hawk, great blue heron, duck, loon, grouse, and osprey; 53 fish including bass, perch, pike, smelt, sturgeon, trout, walleye; and 10 reptiles and amphibians.

Forests cover the Voyagers National Park land, thriving on a thin layer of soil that has formed since the last glaciers melted some 10,000 years ago. The park is in the southern part of the Canadian Shield. You can touch some of the most ancient rock on earth according to the National Park Service, U.S. Department of the Interior. They are older than those found at the bottom of the Grand Canyon.

Eighteenth-century French-Canadian traders, trappers, and Ojibwe Indians paddled birch bark canoes full of trade goods or animal pelts on their way from Rainy Lake to Lake Athabasca, Canada. The Voyagers National Park commemorates a portion of that historic fur trade route. Like in the beginning, the trip is still an adventure.

Voyageurs National Park is approximately five hours north of Minneapolis/St. Paul by car on I-35 and Highway 53, three hours north of Duluth on Highway 53 and four hours south of Winnipeg, Manitoba, Canada. There is no entrance fee. There is no public transportation to the park. International Falls has a small airport with rental cars and taxi service. The National Park Service recommends that you read more about important topics such as camping permits, activity fees, safety, bears, food storage, and lodging before visiting the park. Their official website is www.nps.gov.

Rushing white waters at Kettle Falls, Voyageurs National Park. (Photo courtesy Alan Burchell)

Lake Kabetogama
An angler's pristine paradise

Lake Kabetogama is a charming lady, so enticing in her ways and wiles. Is she beautiful as heaven itself; as inviting as blue sky and puffy white clouds? Or will she sulk today and make you look deeper for your pleasure?

The coming of spring on Kabetogama is especially unique because the lake level is lowered during the winter by action of the dam at Kettle Falls. Residents mark the rising level and speculate how high it will be for "the opener." And a lot rides on it, as the higher the better for fishing and docking. The sun drains the capillaries of the snow and chunks of ice fall from their perches where they were formed early in the winter. Open water forms on the sandbars and shorelines where deer come to drink at dusk.

>—*Excerpt from* Seasons to Savor
>Miriam Burchell, Creative Writer
>Kabetogama, Minnesota

Remarks: Alan Burchell, Miriam's husband, is one of the pioneers and historians associated with the region. Like guides, the now retired, Burchells know the good fishing spots, trails, islands, and places to see and stay. They owned and operated the Moosehorn Resort on the breathtaking Lake Kabetogama for 30-plus years. Alan and Miriam encourage vacationers to settle in and explore the simple to navigate wilderness. First-time visitors can ask for them at Moosehorn Resort, now owned by Christy and Jerry Mitchell.

*Miriam and Alan Burchell, historians of Voyageurs National Park.
(Photo courtesy Alan Burchell)*

Lake Kabetogama in Kabetogama, Minnesota, is the largest of the lakes completely contained in Voyageurs National Park. "Kab," as the locals call it, is one of the most scenic glacier formed lakes in the state, with 80 secluded islands covered by aspen, tall white pine, and majestic spruce forests. The islands' wildlife includes osprey, bald eagles, and pelicans. Lake Kabetogama features 68 undeveloped miles out of its 77 miles of rocky, rugged shoreline. Visitors are truly back to nature. The 80-feet-deep, cool, clean waters provide great fishing for walleye, northern pike, small mouth bass, crappie, and jumbo perch. The smaller lakes located in the interior of the Kabetogama peninsula can be reached by hiking to fish for largemouth bass, muskie, and lake trout. Ice fishing in icehouses is very popular on the lakes in the winter months. Ellsworth's Rock

Gardens is the main visitor site on the far shore. (And a dandy picnic site.)

The Kabetogama Lake Association can help with resorts, area information, boat rentals, fishing guides and outfitters (800-524-9085 and www.exploreminnesota.com).

LAKE KABETOGAMA
MOOSEHORN
RESORT
MINNESOTA

*M**innesota's 500 golf courses help make us one of the top "fun places" in America.*

The Boundary Waters (BWCA)
Minnesota's quietly beautiful canoe wilderness area

> Before the Boundary Waters Canoe Area was established in 1964, my wife, Mary, and I vacationed at the Gunflint Lodge, on the Gunflint Trail, in Grand Marais. Our host was Justine Kerfoot, a name synonymous with wilderness-vacations. I was a city kid from Minneapolis, so the log cabin lodging was adventuresome for me. Being raised in Grand Rapids, Mary was more used to the rustic ways. I was also new to canoes, but learned their secret after some paddling drills that Mary put me through. Seeing the International Boundary marker—with a line showing the United States on one side, and Canada on the other—was a historic moment. Over the years Gunflint Lodge has grown in size and amenities, and has become legendary in its own right as a fourth generation lodge located in the Boundary Waters Canoe Area.
>
> *— Author's highlights*

National Geographic calls it one of its 50 Destinations of a Lifetime. And the thousands of outdoor enthusiasts, who have visited the spectacular Boundary Waters bordering Minnesota and Ontario, Canada, would all agree. Many families make it a priority to pass the experience on to new generations.

The Boundary Waters Canoe Area Wilderness (BWCAW) in Northeastern Minnesota is an expansive 1.3 million-acre preserve of lakes, streams, forests, and remote wilderness stretching almost 150 miles. Located within the Superior National Forest, the BWCAW is federally protected as part of the National Wilderness Preservation System and managed by the USDA Forest Service. Established in

1964, the primitive BWCAW has changed little since the glaciers melted leaving cliffs, canyons, incredible rock formations, and the crystal-clear waters. Almost every granite-cut lake is designated as paddle only, with motors not allowed. There are no roads. Overland trails called portages link the 1,175 lakes and streams. Canoes and gear are carried between lakes just as the early Native Americans and voyageurs did traveling these same waters two or more centuries ago.

With over 1,500 miles of paddling routes, 15 hiking trails, and nearly 2,200 designated campsites, the BWCAW annually welcomes more than 250,000 canoeists and visitors from around the world! Entry points are mapped by areas and ranger districts: Cook/LaCroix, Ely/Kawishiwi, Grand Marais/Gunflint, Isabella, and Tofte/Tofte. Permits are required year-round for day and overnight visitor use. You can see maps, make reservations, or check permit issuing stations and availability at the Boundary Waters Canoe Area Wilderness website www.bwcaw.org. Or call 877-550-6777 for more information. Make reservations for campgrounds in Superior National Forest at www.recreation.gov.

Besides the water-based activities of canoeing, kayaking, and fishing, Boundary Waters' recreation is limitless with the exception of no motorized equipment. A fishing paradise in all seasons, the lakes teem with trout, walleye, bass, and northern pike. Remember to use lead-free tackle. Additional activities are camping, multiple-day backpacking, short-day hiking, maybe to Eagle Mountain, the highest peak in Minnesota (2,301 feet), rock climbing, or swimming. There are sandy beaches. Other nature pursuits include photographing wildflowers in the spring, or scenic landscapes and wildlife all year round, bird watching, star gazing, or picking blueberries, raspberries, and wild cherries. Winter sports include

Canoeist surrounded by quiet wilderness at the Boundary Waters in northeastern Minnesota. (Photo courtesy Explore Minnesota Tourism.)

snowshoeing, cross-country and downhill skiing, skijoring with your dog, dogsledding, ice fishing, and skating. Snowmobiling is permitted outside of the BWCAW. Winter temperatures reach on average 15 to 20 degrees Fahrenheit. Snowfall is 50 to 60 inches.

Among the vast forests of pine, birch, and aspen, and lakes rimmed by woodland, there is a good chance of spotting wildlife. There are moose, deer, bears, bobcats, lynx, loons, and gray wolves, rare to see even with the largest stable wolf population of all the states except Alaska, but you might hear them howling. The American Bird Conservancy recognizes the Superior National Forest as one of the 100 Globally Important Bird Areas. With over 155 nesting species, you will see and hear songbirds, shorebirds, and birds of prey including falcons, owls and bald eagles, the most in the lower 48 states. 79% of the wildlife in the BWCAW is birds, and it has the greatest number of breeding birds in any national forest.

Canoe outfitters at the edge of the BWCA provide adventure trips, canoeing and camping gear, food and cooking supplies, permits and route planning, advice, and expertise. There are outfitters in Ely, Crane Lake, Babbitt, and Grand Marais along the Gunflint Trail, and the Sawbill Trail at Tofte. A services directory is in the official BWCAW Trip Planning publication available from the Forest Supervisor's Office (8901 Grand Avenue Place, Duluth; 218-626-4300; www.fs.fed.us).

Plan your wilderness adventure and travel lightly. Follow BWCAW rules and regulations. Be safe: use a compass and maps, wear lifejackets, do not "run" the rapids, treat water for drinking, avoid dehydration by drinking water frequently, layer clothing to prevent hypothermia, carry a first-aid kit, help reduce fire risk, keep a clean campsite, and practice proper food storage to discourage bears.

The Superior National Forest surrounding the Gunflint Trail has hiking trails, mountain bike trails, boat landings, spots for picking wild blueberries, rustic campgrounds, and 700 miles of winter snowmobile trails (please "Tread Lightly"). A ranger station in Grand Marais provides information on recreation and wildlife in the Superior National Forest (2020 W. Highway 61, Grand Marais; 218-387-1750; Open daily, May 1–September 30; 7:00 a.m.–5:00 p.m., after Labor Day, 8:00 a.m.–4:30 p.m.).

Along the Gunflint Trail, there are about two dozen lodges, resorts, and bed-&-breakfast inns. They provide the opportunity for a comfortable stay in this quiet, peaceful wilderness. You can get more information from the Gunflint Trail Association (800-338-6932 or www.gunflint-trail.com).

When you visit the Boundary Waters Canoe Area, use the *"Leave No Trace"* principle to minimize your impact. *"Plan ahead and prepare, travel and camp on durable surfaces, dispose of waste properly, leave what you find, minimize campfire impacts, respect wildlife and be considerate of other visitors."* The U.S. Forest Service, U.S. Fish & Wildlife Service, National Parks Service, and Bureau of Land Management endorse these practices and work in partnership with The Leave No Trace Center for Outdoor Ethics (www.int.org for more information). Your involvement is vital to insure *"for the American people of present and future generations the benefits of an enduring resource of wilderness"* as called for in the Wilderness Act of 1964 by our United States Congress.

Itasca State Park
The magnificent Mississippi starts here

> When I first saw Itasca State Park as a kid, I did not realize its significance. It was years later when I revisited the headwaters and stepped across the Mississippi that I understood the magnificence of it all.
>
> — *Author's highlights*

The Mississippi River's name is derived from an Ojibwe Indian word meaning "Great River." The name "Itasca" is a Latin word for "truth" and "head." The world's third largest river begins here as a small stream at the headwaters site. It is appropriate that Itasca State Park, near Park Rapids, is Minnesota's first state park, adding to the importance of the Mississippi River's 2,320-mile run to the Gulf of Mexico. Lake Itasca is surrounded by 32,000 acres of beautiful woods with over 100 lakes to add to its breathtaking charm. The area offers a variety of historical and tourist attractions.

The diversity of vegetation in the park supports many wildlife species. Birding is excellent, and visitors are encouraged to help spot and record the bird life they see in the park. Birds include loons, grebes, herons, ducks, owls, hummingbirds, woodpeckers, chickadees, finches, and warblers. Trails in Itasca Park are shared with deer, chipmunks, squirrels, beavers, porcupines, black bears, and wolves.

The famous American geographer and geologist, Henry Schoolcraft determined Lake Itasca to be the Mississippi River's source in 1832.

It was added to the National Register of Historic Places in 1973. The great historic site attracts a half-million visitors annually. Make it your destination in the near future.

*The Mississippi River Headwaters, Lake Itasca.
(Photo courtesy Visit Bemidji)*

State Record Fish
We would like to add your catch to these winners

Species	Weight	Length	Lake & County	Date
Bass (Large Mouth)	8-15	23.5	Lake Auburn/ Carver	10/3/2005
Bass (Small Mouth)	8-0	n/a	West Battle Lake/ Otter Tail	1948
Bluegill	2-13	n/a	Alice Lake/ Hubbard	1948
Crappie (Black)	5-0	21	Vermillion River/ Dakota	1940
Muskellunge	54-0	56	Lake Winnibigoshish/ Itasca	1957
Perch (Yellow)	3-4	n/a	Lake Plantagenette/Hubbard	1945
Pike, Northern	45-12	n/a	Basswood Lake/ Lake	5/16/1929
Trout (Brook)	6-5.6	24	Pigeon River/Cook	9/2/2000
Trout (Brown)	16-12	31.4	Lake Superior/ St. Louis	6/23/1989
Trout (Lake)	43-8	n/a	Lake Superior/ Cook	5/30/1955
Trout (Rainbow)	16-6	33-0	Devil Track River/ Cook	4/27/1980
Walleye	17-8	35.8	Seagull River/Cook	5/13/1979

If California girls are so special—according to the Beach Boys' famous song, "California Girls"—why did Ted Williams, a San Diego boy, marry a girl from Princeton, Minnesota?

Terry Mackenthun, guest of Bowen Lodge, Deer River, with his walleye catch from Lake Winnibigoshish. (Photo courtesy Bowen Lodge)

Top Ten Campgrounds
Load up those Airstreams, RVs, and pickups

Minnesota has campgrounds for every taste. Throughout the state, there is a wide selection of campsites for RVs, campers, and tents. Most are on a lake or river. In addition to the 72 state park campgrounds, there are some five hundred privately owned campgrounds. Further, there are still more sites operated by cities and counties. Here is just a sampling of the beautiful state park campgrounds:

1. Itasca State Park, Park Rapids
2. Boundary Waters Canoe Area (BWCA), northeastern Minnesota
3. Split Rock Lighthouse State Park, Two Harbors
4. Scenic State Park, Bigfork
5. Glendalough State Park, Battle Lake
6. Forestville/Mystery Cave State Park, Wykoff
7. Moose Lake State Park, Moose Lake
8. Nerstrand-Big Woods State Park, Nerstrand
9. Blue Mounds State Park, Luverne
10. Great River Bluffs State Park, Winona

Historic rocks offer an ideal campsite for visitors at the Boundary Waters Canoe Area. (Photo courtesy Explore Minnesota Tourism)

Duluth's Lake Superior
Gateway to the North Shore and the world

Half the ships in and out of Duluth are U.S. or Canadian vessels while the other half are foreign, or as we call them, "salties," because they travel in saltwater, and hail from around the globe.

The most exciting part about working in Duluth is [working with] the salties. I might go on a vessel flagged from the Bahamas with a Polish captain and Russian crew. The next vessel might be a Cyprus-flagged ship with a Filipino crew and a Ukrainian cook. The Greek ships are known for the excellent coffee on board. The master of every ship must speak English in order to enter U.S. waters. And each vessel entering our waters must undergo an annual Coast Guard inspection, including fire drills, man-overboard drills, steering test, and propulsion test.

—*Kevin Rofidal, Edina, Minnesota*

Remarks: Kevin Rofidal, an Edina police officer who is a U.S. Coast Guard Reservist, is assigned to the Marine Safety Unit (MSU) in Duluth, which is responsible for supervising pollution controls and vessel movement and safety.

Kevin Rofidal, U.S. Coast Guard Reservist, on the Roger Blough, Duluth Harbor. (Photo courtesy Kevin Rofidal)

Lake Superior, the largest of the five Great Lakes is fed by 336 rivers; Lake Superior is the largest freshwater lake in the world. It has a surface area of 31,700 square miles with depths of 483 to 1333 feet and measures 350 feet long by 160 feet wide. The scenic shoreline covers 2,726 miles.

Even with its waters being frozen for nearly three months a year, Duluth/Superior ranks as the seventeenth busiest port in the nation, through which passes many tons of bulk cargo, including grain, taconite, fertilizer, pyrite, and rock.

The Aerial Lift Bridge, Duluth's most famous landmark, was originally built in 1905 and renovated in 1929. It takes two minutes to rise and two minutes to lower and goes up over 5,500 times during the shipping season.

Visitors love to spend time exploring seafaring history in Duluth's restored waterfront Canal Park by Lake Superior. The area has cobblestone streets, wrought-iron lampposts, and horse-drawn carriages to take tourists between lakefront hotels and old warehouses now made into shopping and entertainment venues.

Other attractions include the SS William A. Irvin Ore Boat Museum; The Great Lakes Aquarium, a two-story 120,000 gallons interactive freshwater aquarium; Duluth Children's Museum; The Duluth Depot and Lake Superior Railroad Museum; Glensheen Historic Estate, a 39-room mansion built in 1905–08 for Chester and Clara Congdon; Spirit Mountain Ski Resort, with 175 skiable acres, 22 runs and 22 km of cross country ski trails.

Annual events include Grandma's Marathon (June), John Beargrease Sled Dog Marathon (January), Amsoil Duluth National Snocross (November), the Duluth Airshow (July), the Bayfront Reggae Festival (July), and the Duluth Maritime Festival (August).

Duluth visitors also like to take the North Shore Scenic Drive on Highway 61, following Lake Superior for 150 miles between Duluth and the Canadian border. On the way is Gooseberry State Park and a visitor center. It features spectacular waterfalls, Lake Superior shoreline, and a scenic river gorge. The park includes hiking, cross-country and snowmobile trails, and great trout fishing. Further north is the most photographed spot in Minnesota—Split Rock Lighthouse. The popular lighthouse in Split Rock Lighthouse State Park is a historical monument. It offers a breathtaking view of Lake Superior.

Bikers in the Ride/Stride the Divide Mountain Bike Race at Buena Vista Ski Area. (Photo courtesy Visit Bemidji)

Mr. North Woods' Hot Spots
Arrowhead and Iron Range

> Dennis "Denny" Brown lives in Itasca County among northern Minnesota's natural wonders, and he is my nomination for "Mr. North Woods." His backyard adjoins the Mississippi River, and many mornings Denny catches his share of bass for breakfast. A native of Grand Rapids, the state's heartland of 10,000 Lakes, Denny is the former regional director for the Arrowhead Economic Opportunity Agency (jobs and training department). Denny traveled extensively throughout the seven-county Arrowhead region. Further, he is chair of the Central School Commission for the City of Grand Rapids and a member of the Itasca County Historical Society.
>
> Old Central School, built in 1895 and listed on the National Historic Registry, is located at the intersection of Highway 2 and Highway 169 in Grand Rapids. It is home to the Central School Commission, the Itasca County Historical Society, and its Heritage Museum where you can view Minnesota's official State Photograph "Grace," the world-renown portrait taken in 1918, by Eric Enstrom from the small city of Bovey on the byway to the incredible Scenic State Park.
>
> — *Author's highlights*

The following list highlights Denny's favorite places in the Arrowhead area and the Range. Their seven counties include Aitkin, Carlton, Cook, Itasca, Koochiching, Lake, and St. Louis.

Denny and Linda Brown at Lake Superior. (Photo courtesy Denny Brown)

Fishing

- Cut Foot Sioux Lake at Williams Narrows (Chippewa National Forest)
- The Mississippi River in front of my house (in Grand Rapids) and south of the Blandin Paper Mill (The river has dozens of species of fish, and luckily, I have caught them all.)

Hunting

- Mallard Bay. Excellent duck, grouse, and deer hunting. The Bowstring River and Popple River join at Dora Lake; they exit at the north end of Dora Lake as the Bigfork River, then on to Canada. Mallard Bay consists of five bays full of wild rice.

- White Oak. Great duck hunting. This large marsh area is directly south of Deer River and has the Mississippi River flowing through it. One of the earliest fur trading posts was at White Oak Point. Schoolcraft State Park on the Mississippi is nearby. If you get lost in White Oak, look for the water tower in Deer River.

Bait shop

- Ben's Bait Shop, Grand Rapids

Picnicking

- Itasca State Park near Bigfork

Sightseeing

- The Iron Range, Hull Rust Mine in Hibbing (the world's largest iron ore open pit), the Hill Annex Mine tours in Calumet, and Ironworld in Chisholm
- Split Rock Lighthouse on Lake Superior in Lake County
- Jay Cooke State Park in Carlton County

Restaurants

- Forest Lake Restaurant, Grand Rapids (great steakhouse)
- Saw Mill Inn, Grand Rapids (terrific Sunday brunch)
- Valentini's Supper Club, Chisholm (best Italian food in Minnesota)

Golf

- Pokegama Golf Course on Lake Pokegama, Grand Rapids (Pokegama is an Ojibwe term for lake with many bays, or arms, branching out.)

Madden's on Gull Lake

Skiing

- Giants Ridge Golf and Ski Resort, Biwabik (popular spot for every kind of skiing)

Snowmobiling

- The Taconite Trail from Grand Rapids to Ely (a favorite among the Range people; very scenic)

Camping

- Canoe the Bigfork River 44 miles from Little American Falls to Johnson's Landing (You are in a different element; no sign of human intrusion. A great escape, if you can leave your cell phone for a while.)

Resorts

- High Banks Resort, Deer River (on Lake Winnibigoshish, built in the late 1920s by I. B. Nelson)
- Bowen Lodge & Campground, Deer River (on Lake Winnibigoshish)
- Williams Narrows Resort, Cut Foot Sioux Lake

Casino

- Fortune Bay Resort Casino on Lake Vermillion, at Tower (It has a great golf course, marina, and the Bois Forte Heritage Museum.)

Summer festivals and special events

- Dylan Days, Hibbing—May
- Grandma's Marathon, Duluth—June
- Riverboat Heritage Days, Aitkin—July (The steamboats came to Grand Rapids; the farthest point they can travel.)
- Blueberry Art Festival, Ely—July

- White Oak Rendezvous, Deer River—August
- Itasca County Fair, Grand Rapids—August
- Judy Garland Festival, Grand Rapids—August
- Tall Timber Days Festival, Grand Rapids—August

Gift and souvenir shops

- Old Central School, Grand Rapids (Quilt Shop, Stain Glass Shop, Yarn Shop; home to the Itasca County Historical Society)
- Reed Drug Store, Grand Rapids
- Border Bob's, International Falls
- Canelake's Homemade Candies, Virginia

Ten Favorite Bait Shops
Stop in and learn where they are biting

1. **God's Country Outfitters,** Grand Rapids
2. **Lundeen's Tackle Castle,** Mille Lacs Lake
3. **Ike's Bait and Tackle,** Red Wing
4. **Log Cabin and Tackle,** Baudette
5. **In Towne Marina,** Waconia
6. **Fred's Bait,** Deer River
7. **Voyageur North Canoe Outfitters,** Ely
8. **Lindy Little Joe,** Brainerd
9. **Tebers Bait Shop,** Bemidji
10. **Marine General,** Lake Superior

Mary Osborne, Boone, Iowa, guest at Shing Wako Resort on Lake Edward, Merrifield. (Photo courtesy Jim Schleisman)

Top Ten Metro Parks
Plan your next outing at one of these spots

The Twin Cities area's nationally renowned system of parks contributes significantly to our high quality of life. The system includes 46 regional parks and preserves, 22 trails, and six special recreation areas. Some have preserves for wildlife watching; others are great for fishing, swimming, biking, and hiking; all work for picnicking:

1. **Minnehaha Falls Park,** Minneapolis
2. **Hyland-Bush-Anderson Lakes Park Reserve,** Bloomington
3. **Lake Minnetonka Regional Park,** Minnetrista
4. **Como Park Zoo & Conservatory,** St. Paul
5. **Lake of the Isles,** Minneapolis
6. **Lake Calhoun,** Minneapolis
7. **Lake Harriet,** Minneapolis
8. **Lake Nokomis,** Minneapolis
9. **Bryant Lake Regional Park,** Eden Prairie
10. **Bunker Hills Regional Park,** Coon Rapids

Lake Calhoun is the center attraction for the Minneapolis Aquatennial's Milk Carton Boat Races every July. (Photo courtesy Minneapolis Aquatennial)

Chapter Three
Dining & Places to Go

MOA (Mall of America)
One of America's top tour attractions

> I grew up in Bloomington with my two sisters, Kathy and Janet. We lived on a hill with 10 acres. [There was] lots of wildlife around then. We had a picnic table, basketball hoop, swing set, and playhouse. We loved sliding down the hill in winter. It was a wonderful place to grow up. We got to pick strawberries from a nearby field—and were paid for it by Ed Chadwick, a storeowner and community leader. We attended Oak Grove Presbyterian Church. I saw The Beatles live at old Met Stadium. People reported they could hear the concert music a mile away. Now I live in Thunder Bay, Canada. And the good part, Minneapolis is only seven hours away, so I come back often to see family, friends, and the Mall of America.
>
> —Nancy Blake Knauff
> Thunder Bay, Ontario, Canada

People from all over the world come to marvel at the Taj Mahal of shopping. The Mall of America attracts more annual visitors than Disney World, Graceland, and the Grand Canyon combined.

Minnesota is a leader in retailing. Southdale Shopping Center in Edina, built in 1956, was the nation's first indoor shopping mall.

In 1992, the Mall of America, the largest retail and entertainment complex in the nation, opened in Bloomington, 15 minutes away from Southdale.

MOA boasts 520 specialty stores, 50 restaurants, 7 nightclubs, and 14 movie theaters. And if that is not enough, it features the first Nickelodeon Universe theme park, the largest indoor park in the

Visitors come nose to nose with 4,500 sharks and other sea creatures at the MOA's Underwater Adventure's Aquarium. (Photo courtesy Mall of America)

nation. The Mall features four major anchor stores: Bloomingdale's, Macy's, Nordstrom, and Sears.

More than 4,000 couples from around the world have exchanged marriage vows in The Chapel of Love Wedding Chapel.

Hundreds of walkers use the 4.2 million-square-foot Mall of America daily for exercise and socialization. The Walksport Mall Stars walking club includes 4,000 registered walkers.

The MOA features special events that offer free entertainment. For example, many of the local radio and TV stations broadcast right from the mall's atrium and involve visitors in their programs.

And do not go home without seeing the Underwater Adventures Aquarium, a 1.2 million gallon walk-through aquarium. Its education value is priceless.

Nowhere will you ever see as many kiosks, all filled to the brims. And remember there is no sales tax on clothing bought in Minnesota.

North Dakota-born Lawrence Welk attended MacPhail Music School, Minneapolis, in the 1920s (Now MacPhail Music Center). They taught him well, as the "Ah-one, Ah-two" band leader went on to host one of the longest running shows in TV history.

Hidden Treasures
Ask the residents for the local flavor

We all have been stumped when in a new area with what to do and where to go. The easiest solution is to ask the locals.

- **The General Store,** Minnetonka—Lots of Minnesota-made gifts, souvenirs, and goods are available here in endless variety. It is a multilevel 20,000-square-foot, charming store with unique gift items and home decor. Stay for lunch in its cafe for salads, made-to-order sandwiches, soup, and delicious desserts. The General Store is at 4401 Highway 7 in Minnetonka just west of I-494 (952-935-7131, www.generalstoreofminnetonka.com).
- **American Swedish Institute,** Minneapolis—The museum displays the institute's collection of Swedish glass, decorative and fine arts, textiles, and items from Sweden. The permanent exhibit "Swedish Life in the Twin Cities," explores the local Swedish-American community through photographs, diaries, vintage recordings and immigrant artifacts. The gift shop is the place to find imported Swedish and Scandinavian gifts and books. On the National Register of Historic Places, the American Swedish Institute is the only castle in the Twin Cities. American Swedish Institute at 2600 Park Avenue in Minneapolis (612-871-4907, www.americanswedishinst.org).
- **Covington Inn,** St. Paul—A bed and breakfast on the water offers a quiet getaway with city life. It is one of America's few floating B & Bs, docked across the Mississippi River from downtown St. Paul. It makes a special wedding ceremonial site, too. Covington Inn is at 100 Harriet Island Road B3 in St. Paul (612-292-1411, www.covingtoninn.com).

- **Nancy Nelson's Our Little Secret,** Minneapolis—Your chance to meet a TV star while you find designer accessories at wholesale prices. Nancy Nelson, the infomercial queen, is on hand to greet you while you admire the watches, jewelry, home decor, luggage, and lots of fashion fun. What is the secret? Nancy says no one will ever know how little you spent. Our Little Secret is at 6001 Lyndale Avenue South, directly across from Bachman's (612-869-8290, www.ourlittlesecret.tv).
- **Emma Krumbee's,** Belle Plaine—Home of the Annual Great Scarecrow Festival, Emma Krumbee's Orchard and Farm has fun and exciting activities for everyone all year long. The restaurant offers fantastic country meals, and there is an excellent gift store, too. It is only 45 minutes from Minneapolis or Mankato. Emma Krumbee's at Highway 169, 501 East South Street in Belle Plaine (952-873-3006, www.emmakrumbees.com).
- **United States Hockey Hall of Fame,** Eveleth—The Museum exhibits and films feature the 1960 and 1980 "Miracle on Ice" Olympic gold medal teams. (Who would have thought we would beat the Russians?) The "Capital of American Hockey" is a great place to meet world-class hockey players, coaches, and fans and learn more about Minnesota's rich history in Eveleth's favorite sport. Better than a hat trick, is the world's largest hockey stick (107 feet long), and 700-pound hockey puck—all located at the U.S. Hockey Hall of Fame, 801 Hat Trick Avenue in Eveleth (800-443-7825, www.ushockeyhall.com).
- **Red Wing Pottery,** Red Wing—Prepare to spend some time watching the famous Red Wing Pottery being made, and to see all the selections of crocks, pitchers, mugs, dinnerware,

and other pieces. Like a small shopping center, it has other gift store offerings, including old-fashioned candy. It can make special pottery pieces as a premium or memento for a reunion or business meeting. Red Wing Pottery is located on the banks of the Mississippi River in beautiful Red Wing. Red Wing Pottery is at 1920 West Main Street in Red Wing (800-228-0174, www.redwingpottery.com).

- **Pavek Museum of Broadcasting,** St. Louis Park—Here is the world's finest collection of antique radio, television, and broadcast equipment. Children can actually create their own radio broadcasts in an authentic 1960s-era studio, and people of all ages can enjoy a variety of classic programs and interviews with local broadcast pioneers. Also, see the Pavek Museum's Minnesota Broadcasting Hall of Fame that inducted many WCCO Radio alumni: Cedric Adams, Clellan Card, Charlie Boone, Roger Erickson, Joyce Lamont, and Howard Viken. Pavek Museum of Broadcasting is at 3515 Raleigh Avenue in St. Louis Park (952-926-8198, www.pavekmuseum.org).

- **LARK Toys,** Kellogg—This small town in southeastern Minnesota is the home of the largest independent toy store in the country. LARK Toys store features exclusive wood crafted toys, blocks, rockers, dollhouses, and puzzles designed by owner Donn Kreofsky. L.A.R.K. stands for Lost Arts Revival by Kreofsky, a fitting name for a small family company dedicated to bringing back wood-crafted toys. In addition, the store carries international wooden, developmental, and tin wind-up toys, pedal cars, and books selected by Donn's wife, Sarah, a former schoolteacher. And fun for the whole family. It also contains a one-of-a-kind working carousel made with 19 hand-carved animals, the Rocking Café, a bakery, coffee-shop, party room, and antique toy museum. LARK Toys is located 80 miles from the Twin Cities overlooking the scenic river bluffs on LARK Lane, Kellogg (507-767-3387, www.larktoys.com).

Judy Garland Museum
The Land of Oz moves to Minnesota

> I first saw Judy's house in 1955 when visiting Grand Rapids with my wife, Mary. She and her family lived across the alley from Judy. Good friends of my wife's, the Marion Browns with their two boys, Tom and Denny, lived in the house until it was moved and turned into a museum.
>
> My wife's dad, Ray Connell, used to babysit baby Francis Ethel Gumm, (Judy's birth name.) He remembered Judy's first public stage performance at age three in her father's new Grand Theater. She sang "Jingle Bells," and made quite a hit. Judy and her two sisters performed their act throughout Minnesota before moving to California in 1926.
>
> *— Author's highlights*

There is no place like home! Judy Garland's home, that is, and it has been restored into the Judy Garland Museum in Grand Rapids. Like a national treasure, thousands of people make the pilgrimage each summer to the popular northern tourist town for their Judy "fix."

Minnesota's own, Judy Garland. (Photo courtesy Judy Garland Museum)

Guests can tour the restored 1920s house and the adjacent museum that displays thousands of items from Judy's career. The original two-story house was moved from the heart of town to the museum site on Highway 169, just south of downtown Grand Rapids.

George Jessel gets credit for changing the Gumm name to Garland at the Oriental Theatre in Chicago during the 1934 World's Fair. Unimpressed with the sisters as a singing trio, MGM wisely culled out Judy and gave her a contract in 1935. The rest is history.

There is a lot to see and reminisce from those great Judy Garland days. Besides the famous ruby slippers from her signature movie, *The Wizard of Oz*, there are historic photos, costumes, and wonderful memories of the MGM star. Judy's song, "Over the Rainbow," thought to be one of the greatest songs of the twentieth century, can be enjoyed at the museum. And for those who want to bring home some of those precious mementos, there is a nifty gift shop.

Few go home without picking up DVDs of Judy's movies. According to critics, the irresistible team of Judy Garland and Mickey Rooney was as great as Laurel and Hardy, Jeanette MacDonald and Nelson Eddy, or William Powell and Myrna Loy.

The Judy Garland Museum, Grand Rapids, showcases hundreds of mementos, including the famous Ruby Slippers from MGM's The Wizard of Oz.
(Photo courtesy Judy Garland Museum)

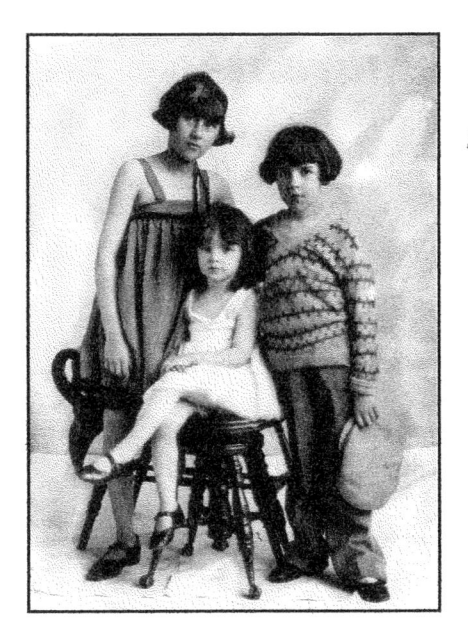

Always the center of attention, Judy Garland, (on stool), with "The Gumm Sisters," as their act was billed in 1927. (Photo courtesy Judy Garland Museum)

And if there is a wedding in your plans, you can have it performed in Judy's own parlor.

The Judy Garland Museum: 2727 US Highway 169 South in Grand Rapids, 800-664-5839, www.judygarlandmuseum.com.

Judy Garland's Best Movies

- *The Wizard of Oz*
- *Meet Me in St. Louis*
- *The Harvey Girls*
- *Good Old Summertime*
- *For Me and My Gal*
- *Easter Parade*
- *A Star is Born*
- *Summer Stock*
- *The Pirate*
- *Judgment at Nuremberg*

Top Ten Restaurants
Minnesota offers a smorgasbord of dining

Just as sure as night follows day, you are going to be served lutefisk when you are among Scandinavians during the holidays. Their fish specialty dish is not as bad it sounds, but yes, it is true that cooking lutefisk chases many people out of the house. My wife, Mary, is Swedish, but instead of making the Christmas delicacy at home—she has thankfully agreed to let someone else cook it. Now we go out to Pearson's Edina Restaurant. And so she doesn't suffer alone eating the lutefisk, I order it too. As proof, our server once gave me a button that reads "Pearson's Lutefisk Experience." So, Uff da! Lutefisk. I am glad that is over with, and now I can get back to those Swedish meatballs.

— Author's highlights
A button award for ordering lutefisk at Pearson's
Restaurant, Edina (Author's collection)

1. **Pearson's Edina Restaurant**, Edina— Pearson's is a charming neighborhood café known for great home cooking. The Scandinavian hospitality adds to your visit. Swedish meatballs are one of the favorites, served with mashed potatoes, gravy, vegetable, and salad. (Be sure to order the squash.) Great spot for breakfast, too. Both the pancakes and waffles will have you coming back. Experience lutefisk and lefse during the holidays at 3808 West 50th Street, one block east of France Avenue on in Edina (612-927-4464, www.PearsonsEdinaRestaurant.org).
2. **LaCasita Mexican Restaurant**, Roseville—All the traditional Mexican specialties served in a south of the border

atmosphere decorated with hand-painted murals on plastered walls—a unique ambiance that adds to your meal. LaCasita features one of the largest selections of premium tequilas in the region and has 18 flavors available for your margarita. The restaurant is perfect for family dining, visiting with friends, entertaining business associates, or celebrating Cinco de Mayo. Columbia Heights (since 1984), St. Cloud (future site), and in Roseville at 1925 Perimeter Road (651-287-4055, www.lacasita.biz).

3. **Ruth's Chris Steak House**, Minneapolis—From humble beginnings in New Orleans, Ruth's Chris Steak House claims it is the world's largest fine-dining company. Its Signature Steaks are sealed to perfection at 1,800 degrees and topped with fresh butter so they sizzle all the way to your table. They also feature delicious sides and desserts worth eating first. Elegant surroundings, located in the International Center II, at 920 2nd Avenue South, Suite 100, downtown Minneapolis (612-672-9000, www.ruthschris.com/Steak-House). Call for reservations.

4. **Perkins Restaurant & Bakery**, I-494 and France, Bloomington—Here is one of the larger and fancier Perkins. The menu offers hungry guests a comprehensive breakfast, lunch, and dinner selection ranging from the traditional to the innovative. And an added bonus is the in-house *bake shoppe* where you can either order or take out a wide array of freshly baked muffins, pies, and cookies. It requires key ingredients to be successful in the restaurant business for more than 40 years—and Perkins seems to have the right recipe. 4201 W. 78th Street, Bloomington (952-831-8855, www.perkinsrestaurants.com).

5. **Great India Restaurant**, Brooklyn Center—It offers distinctive cuisine in an informal, friendly setting. Great India

enjoys a reputation for impeccable service, elegant décor, and exquisite Indian food. Whether you are planning parties, buffets, business luncheons, or a lively family reunion, Great India can accommodate you. The menu also features a selection of vegetarian and light dishes to cater to every dietary need. 6056 Shingle Creek Parkway, Brooklyn Center (763-560-8480, www.greatindiarestaurant.us).

6. **Kozy's Steaks and Seafood**, Edina—The founders of Jax Café in northeast Minneapolis have started a new tradition of great food in Edina. The menu features fresh-made soups, daily specials, classic steakhouse fare, fresh seafood, and tempting appetizers. They provide a comfortable setting for a quick lunch, after work stress-release, brunch, or the perfect place to celebrate that special dinner. Located at the SE corner of the Galleria Shopping Center, 3220 Galleria, Edina (952-224-5866, www.kozysteakandseafood.com). Call for reservations.

7. **Famous Dave's**, five locations, including Minnetonka and MOA—Dave's St. Louis style barbecue ribs are smoked to perfection and topped with Dave's award-winning Rich & Sassy sauce, also found in food stores. The menu boasts tongue tickling chicken, char-grilled burgers, and fish. Sides include corn on the cob, a treat any time of year. Guests love the down-home atmosphere. Eat in, take out, or have your party catered—Dave's does it all. 14601 Highway 7, Minnetonka (952-933-9600, www.famousdaves.com).

8. **Kincaid's**, Bloomington—Featuring fish, chops, and steaks. The rock salt-roasted prime rib is famous, but steaks are great if the restaurant runs out. You will be attracted to the twinkling white lights, greenery, and bubbling built-in stream that create a romantic evening setting. Expect a

dressed-up crowd (suits and even some jewels), with an occasional jeans-clad diner. Reservations are recommended for this award-winning restaurant. Located on the main floor of an office building at 8400 Normandale Lake Boulevard (952-921-2255, www.kincaids.com).

9. **David Fong's Restaurant**, Bloomington—A Twin Cities favorite for great Chinese and American cuisine. Specialties include New York Steak Chinatown, shrimp Hong Kong, Fong's house chicken, and chow mein. David Fong's is the longest operated family-owned restaurant in Bloomington (And for decades a Chinese community leader). They offer private lunches and dinner, and company functions. 9329 Lyndale Avenue South, Bloomington (952-888-9294, www.davidfongs.com).

10. **The Buffet, Mystic Lake Casino**, Prior Lake—An international culinary adventure awaits you at The Buffet, the largest casino buffet in the Midwest. Tempt your taste buds with your favorite dishes from around the globe, including carved prime rib, fresh seafood, hearth-baked pizzas, Chicken Kiev, and Moo Goo Gai Pan. Indulge yourself at the dessert station—with everything from tempting pastries to towering sundaes and gourmet coffees. In the Mystic Lake Casino, 2400 Mystic Lake Boulevard, Prior Lake (952-496-7243, www.mysticlake.com).

For a memorable birthday, celebrate at Pearson's Restaurant and hear "Happy Birthday" sung in Swedish. Your gift will be a free slice of delicious cake.

Best Shopping
Minnesota is America's shopping center

To get you off and running, here is a partial list of the places for special merchandise:

Malls

- **Mall of America,** Bloomington
- **Brookdale,** Brooklyn Center
- **Burnsville Center,** Burnsville
- **Eden Prairie Center,** Eden Prairie
- **Galleria,** Edina
- **Southdale,** Edina
- **Shops at Arbor Lake,** Maple Grove
- **Maplewood Mall,** Maplewood
- **Calhoun Square,** Minneapolis
- **Gavidae Common,** Minneapolis
- **City Center,** Minneapolis
- **Ridgedale,** Minnetonka
- **Rosedale Center,** Roseville
- **Woodbury Lakes,** Woodbury

Outlets

- **Albertville Premium Outlets,** Albertville
- **Tanger Factory Outlets,** North Branch
- **Medford Outlet Center,** Medford
- **Pinnacle Village Outlets** (2009), Bemidji

Shopping Districts

- **Grand Avenue shops,** St. Paul
- **50th & France shops,** Edina
- **Downtown Wayzata,** Wayzata
- **White Bear Lake,** White Bear
- **Nicollet Mall,** Downtown Minneapolis
- **Uptown,** Minneapolis
- **Linden Hills,** Minneapolis
- **Stillwater shops,** Stillwater

Specialty Shops

- **Hoigaard's,** St. Louis Park. The Hoigaard family has provided quality merchandise and excellent customer-focused service since 1895. The store features skiing, snowboarding, camping, canoeing, hiking, biking, inline skating equipment and related clothing, and porch and patio furniture.
- **Cabela's,** Rogers & Owatonna. Cabela's is the world's largest mail-order, retail, and Internet outfitter for hunting, fishing, camping, and other outdoor related merchandise. Stores also feature museum quality wildlife displays and aquariums.
- **Hopkins Antique Mall,** Hopkins. With two stories and 68 dealers, it is the largest antiques and collectibles mall in the west metro.

Favorite Places
Each scores a perfect "Minnesota Ten"

Good times are plentiful in the metro Twin Cities. Here are some places you will want to explore. Be sure to share your experience with friends and relatives. Or better yet, take them along.

- **Minnesota History Center,** St. Paul
- **Valley Fair,** Shakopee
- **Minnesota Landscape Arboretum,** Chaska
- **Minnesota Zoo,** Apple Valley
- **University of Minnesota,** Minneapolis
- **Chanhassen Dinner Theatres,** Chanhassen
- **Bachman's,** Minneapolis
- **Mall of America,** Bloomington
- **Minnesota Orchestra,** Minneapolis
- **Guthrie Theater,** Minneapolis

They never boast about it, but Bachman's is the world's largest retail florist. And a bonus, that you will enjoy too, is the Patrick's French Bakery/ Restaurant inside the Lyndale Avenue store.

Sarah Jane's Bakery
A small town bakery in the middle of the city

One early morning—it must have been about 4:30 a.m.—I heard Al Malmberg on his all-night talk show on WCCO, Twin Cities. The Lonely Guy, a regular caller, was just finishing his spiel. Half awake, I heard Al raving about the hand-cut donuts Sarah Jane's Bakery had just sent over to the station.

I made a mental note to try them sometime. Another early morning, it was the lemon jellyrolls that he was all excited about. And this time, Sarah Jane was on the air telling about the special they were having on them. And when she mentioned they were like sponge cakes, it got my attention. No hard sell about it. Just two people casually talking about all the great fresh-baked treats that were waiting for the listeners at Sarah Jane's Bakery, at 2853 Johnson Street N.E., Minneapolis.

That sold me. I had to try some for myself. Besides the jellyroll, I went home with some of Sarah Jane's wheat bread, a dozen cookies, and donuts. Good thing I didn't need one of their wedding cakes. They sure looked good.

— *Author's highlights*

Sarah Jane's Bakery has been satisfying customers for well over 30 years. Located at 2853 Johnson Street N.E., Minneapolis along a stretch near I-35W–in an area the locals have dubbed "Nordeast."

They bake from scratch. Everything is made fresh from a recipe. They do not add any preservatives and only use the best, quality ingredients.

Pastries, donuts, deserts, and bread are baked through the evening and served fresh and warm in the morning. Friday mornings offer the best selection.

The small-business owner has a chance for success when offering a product or service that buyers need or want. Krispy Kreme, the giant donut-maker, had no affect on Sarah Jane's Bakery. Its business base is in fact stronger than ever.

Despite the demands of running the bakery, owners Sarah and Kevin Lovgren have always found the time to get involved in helping make their neighborhood a positive place to make a living. They also donate a lot of product. "We don't throw anything away," Lovgren said. "Anything that's left at the end of the day goes to feed families in need. Nothing goes to waste."

Having operated a successful bakery since 1975, the Lovgrens draw on their own business experience to offer the kind of leadership and vision that is so vital for local economies to grow and thrive. "We all need a strong business community to succeed," advised Kevin Lovgren.

Curious Side Trips
Minnesota features hundreds of endearing novelties

Travelers occasionally need to get off the beaten path to find Minnesota's best kept tourist secrets. It is amazing what awaits you. Many of the roadside novelties are free for the looking. Some marvelous gems are housed in museums that may require a small entrance fee. All have their charm and are part of Minnesota's fun journeys.

Side Trips by City

- **The Runestone Museum**, Alexandria—History buffs will enjoy the time spent in this beautiful resort town touted as the birthplace of America, according to the Kensington Runestone legend. You can see the controversial Viking inscribed runic dated 1362 and get the full story about the immigrant farmer, Olaf Ohman, who found the original artifact in 1897. Scientists, geologists, and even linguists from around the world have studied the mysterious Runestone in efforts to authenticate it. You can also tour Fort Alexandria, a replica of the 1862 stockade built by the Eighth Regular Infantry and walk through several pioneer log buildings, an 1880 country school house, and view the Snorri, a wooden 40-foot Viking ship replica. Take a short drive to Kensington Park to see the Ohman family farm and the Runestone's discovery site. The Runestone Gift Shop features Minnesota and local Alexandria souvenirs, plus Viking and Runestone information books. The attraction is in downtown Alexandria at 206 North Broadway (320-763-3999, www.runestonemuseum.org).
- **The SPAM Museum**, Austin—Only in Austin can you find a shrine dedicated to SPAM, the world-famous canned

meat produced by the Hormel Food Corporation. A must for SPAM lovers who can learn what exactly goes into it, the role it played in WWII, and how it became a popular pop culture icon. Located off I-90 exit 178-B in Austin (800-LUV-SPAM, www.spam.com).

- **Giant Twine Ball**, Darwin—See for yourself that hobbies can take all shapes and sizes. Francis A. Johnson wrapped twine for four hours every day for 23 weeks beginning in 1950 and then continued his project for 39 years. The result is a ball of twine 13 feet in diameter, which weighs over 17,000 pounds. It is the largest ball of twine rolled by one person. It was listed in the *Guinness Book of Records* for over 12 years and is recorded in three editions of *Ripley's Believe It or Not*. An enclosed gazebo protects the ball, like a precious jewel, in full view for your camera. The volunteer-run Ball of Twine Museum is on County Road 14, south of Darwin, off Highway 12 (320-693-6651, www.darwintwineball.com).
- **"The Lutefisk Capital of the United States,"** Madison—To welcome visitors, the townspeople of Madison built the world's largest cod fish statue. Later named "Lou T. Fisk" and dedicated in 1983, it is 25 feet long, made of fiberglass, and finished in bright acrylics. Lou T. Fisk has toured around the country as an ambassador for this southwestern prairie city. Lou made Madison famous and distinguished it from Glenwood's often-repeated claim of being the "Lutefisk Capital of the World." Madison's legendary Norsefest, the annual Scandinavian celebration featuring ethnic costumes, dumplings and ham, krumkake, rommegrot, lefse, and lutefisk (made from air-dried whitefish prepared in soda lye) is held in early November. Lou T. Fisk is located in J.F. Jacob-

sen Park on Highway 75, near the intersection of Highways 40 and 75 (320-598-7373, www.ci.madison.mn.us).

- **Paul Bunyan's Fishing Bobber**, Pequot Lakes—In the town square of this city, known for its great fishing lakes, is a gigantic white and bright red water tower shaped just like a bobber. The 60-foot water tower gets the attention of everyone passing by. Local legend has it that the lumberjack Paul Bunyan lost the bobber while casting his pole for the infamous fish Notorious Nate. Once an actual working water tower, the fishing bobber is now a landmark adjacent to the Paul Bunyan State Trail. Pequot Lakes is at mile marker 21 of the 110 mile long multiple use hiking, biking, and snowmobile trail running between Brainerd and Bemidji (800-450-2838, www.explorebrainerdlakes.com).

- **One of the Largest Corncobs in the World**, Rochester—The "Best Small City in America" and home to the Mayo Clinic also boasts one of tallest ears of corn. An eye-catching 150-foot water tower featuring a 60-foot high yellow-and-green corncob built to enlarged scale. This 1931 landmark holds 50,000 gallons of water and is still in use by the Seneca Foods plant. Area farmers do have some of the best cornfields in the state! Located by the intersection of Highways 14 and 63, on the south edge of town (800-634-8277, www.rochestercvb.org).

- **Twelve-Level Tree House**, St. Louis Park—Like its huge supporting oak branches, Mark Tucker's 1986 project just kept growing. Six levels the first year; finished now with an even dozen. A thing of beauty, the 40-foot outdoor showpiece has a view of several miles from the top level. The controversial "Tucker's Tree House" underwent required City building code modifications including upper level ladders, safety cages, and handgrips. Legally, the tree house cannot be expanded. Regular inspections are conducted including forestry inspections for the tree's health. For historical information on the Tree House or other St. Louis Park structures, visit www.slphistory.org. To view the Tree House take Minnetonka Boulevard east off Highway 100 for a few blocks to Ottawa. It is on the left side of the road at 4800 Minnetonka Boulevard, in St. Louis Park. For information about tours, call Mark Tucker at 952-920-6627.

Bikers and hikers love the hundreds of miles of state scenic trails, including the popular 55-mile Central Lakes Trail. It runs through the communities of Osakis, Nelson, Alexandria, Garfield, Brandon, Evansville, Melby, Ashby, and beyond to Fergus Falls.

Chapter Four
Four Seasons of Fun

Festivals & Events
Celebrating our Four Seasons of Fun

Nothing brings people together better than a hometown festival or special event. And the good part is that they are going on all the time. Minnesota puts on more than 800 public happenings each year. Everything from outdoor concerts, country fairs, and art crawls to the Duluth Polar Bear Plunge in Lake Superior. Some festivals feature beauty pageants and hometown parades with all the bells and whistles, including the hometown local high school band. Many spotlight their veterans whom everyone likes to see and honor. Others have a rich tradition, such as the Minnesota State Fair (1859), St. Paul Winter Carnival (1886), and the Minneapolis Aquatennial (1940). Here is a listing of the ongoing events from all over the state:

Most notable

- **St. Paul Winter Carnival**—January
- **Art in Bloom**, Minneapolis Institute of Arts—May
- **Grandma's Marathon**, Duluth—June
- **Minneapolis Aquatennial**—July
- **Taste of Minnesota**, St. Paul—July
- **Farmfest**, Redwood County—August
- **Uptown Art Fair**, Minneapolis—August
- **WE Fest**, Detroit Lakes—August
- **Minnesota State Fair**—late August to early September

- **Minnesota Renaissance Festival,** Shakopee—August through September
- **Anoka's Grand Day Halloween Parade**—October
- **Oktoberfest,** New Ulm—October

Edina Art Fair—June. More than 400 artists from all regions of the United States display their crafts in early June. The popular three-day art fair has children's activities, fashion shows, great food, and lifestyle demonstrations. Stroll the quaint 50th and France Quarter where Minneapolis and Edina meet. Started in 1965, it grows each year. For more information, call 952-922-1524.

Milk Carton Boat Races, Lake Calhoun—July. It is the big splash of summer. The Milk Carton Boat Races are the signature event of the annual Minneapolis Aquatennial celebration. Minnesotans of all ages and skill levels let their imaginations go wild when constructing boats entirely from empty milk cartons. Fun themed races are held, and the judges decide winners by creativity and speed. Each of the people-powered boats is handcrafted with many of the participants spending months on their project. Past years included distinctive designs from canoe shaped to dragons to the Queen Mary. In 1993, a local firm used 25,000 cartons to make a 100-foot aircraft carrier. Held in Minneapolis, at Thomas Beach, Lake Calhoun. For more information, call 612-376-7669 or visit www.aquatennial.org.

Not to be missed

- **Frostbite Festival,** Fergus Falls—February
- **Grumpy Old Men Festival,** Wabasha—February
- **Ice Harvest,** Waseca—February
- **Polar Bear Ice Plunge,** Duluth—February
- **Winter Fest,** Spicer—January–February

- **Annual Fishing Opener and Community BBQ,** Grand Rapids—May
- **Hundreds of Fourth of July Parades,** and 95 county fairs
- **Lake George Blueberry Festival,** Park Rapids—July
- **Potato Days,** Barnesville—August
- **Taste of Dorset,** Dorset—August

World Famous Fish House Parade, Aitkin—November. Parade lovers should put this one on their calendar. It is an eight-block ice fishing house parade and celebration, held in Aitkin the day after Thanksgiving. You will see creative fish house floats, wacky costumes, igloos, the Crappie Queen, celebrities, and athletes, plus every fire engine the town ever owned. The ice fishing houses are destined for use on the 365 frozen lakes around the town. Afterward, attend the American Legion Chili Cook-Off; enjoy hearty helpings of Fish House Stew at the Moose Lodge, or pancake breakfasts and sloppy joe lunches. For more information, call 800-526-8342 or visit www.aitkin.com.

Charitable

St. Patrick's Garage Sale, Edina—September. Here is the mother of all garage sales. People from all over wait anxiously for this Catholic Church-sponsored rummage sale, held for three days in the middle of September. Items from clothes, bikes, furniture, luggage, tools, and small appliances to household items all are available in one gigantic garage-sale atmosphere. Items are reasonably priced. And it is a great place to donate items, too. St. Patrick's Garage Sale at the Church of St. Patrick's, 6820 St. Patrick's Lane in Edina. For more information, call 952-941-3164 or visit www.stpatrick-edina.org.

Hometown marching bands are often part of the annual festivals and events held throughout Minnesota. (Photo courtesy Minnesota State Fair)

- **Annual Climb for a Cure**—February. Cystic Fibrosis Foundation (since 1981)
- **Annual Big Brothers Big Sisters Award Gala**—February. Big Brothers Big Sisters Twin Cities mentoring program (since 1998)
- **Taste of Chocolate**—March. Bloomington Arts Council (since 1995)
- **Annual Pacer Benefit**—April. Pacer benefits children with disabilities (since 1983)
- **Susan G. Kohman Twin Cities Race for the Cure**—May. Dedicated to breast cancer awareness, treatment, and research (since 1993)
- **Orchid Lights**—June. Minnesota Landscape Arboretum Foundation
- **Camp Courage Open**—July. Programs for campers with physical and sensory disabilities (since 1995)
- **Habitat 500**—July. 500-mile bike ride for Habitat for Humanity to build homes for low-income families (since 1993)

- **Twin Cities Polo Classic**—August—Twin City Polo Club, Independence. Benefits Children's Cancer research fund (since 1989)
- **Book Lovers Ball**—October. Milkweed Editions (since 2000)
- **Antiques Show & Sale**—November. Minneapolis Institute of Art (since 1984)
- **Macy's Holidazzle Parade**—November 23 to December 23. Benefits The Emergency Food Shelf Network (since 1992)

Winter Wonderland
Hot chocolate is Minnesotans' antifreeze

Being a kid in Minnesota involved extremes: the juiciest summers with fresh strawberries and raspberries from my dad's garden; the hot dogs and pink cotton candy at the Itasca County Fair in Grand Rapids, the cool lapping waters of the lakes, followed by the numbing, freezing winters when life seemed to stand still, when frost on the inside of the bedroom window was crusty and thick, and my white breath would surround me as I hurried to school, bundled up with so much clothing I could hardly walk. But, being a kid, it was all just a part of a daily kaleidoscope of living well, playing hard, and being in the moment.

—Marjorie Evjen Connell
Anaheim, California

Winter can be cold. However, there is no cabin fever for most Minnesotans. We just bundle up and go out and play in the snow or stay indoors enjoying the warmth of a fireplace and a sip of hot chocolate.

Minnesota's annual snowfall is from 37 to 70 inches, depending on your location. Winter provides the perfect backdrop for skating, sledding, ice fishing, snowshoeing, snowmobiling, and downhill and cross-country skiing. In addition, the snow sets the stage for two popular Twin City winter events: The December Holidazzle event with daily parades in Minneapolis and the St. Paul Winter Carnival, the "Coolest Celebration on Earth," held in late January.

Snowmobiles introduced an exciting new sport and industry to our state, brought a new thrill to winter, and helped extend some resort owners' season. At its peak, there were dozens of snowmobile manufacturers in the nation. Now it is just the Minnesota pioneers, Arctic Cat, and Polaris.

During the holidays, many venture out to their nearby church, school, or college for a Christmas play or concert. Some are lucky enough to hear the talented St. Olaf choir in Northfield, which with 75 mixed voices, is one of the best *a cappella* choirs in the United States. The choir keeps busy with its recordings, Christmas Festival, and world tours. Another top choir is at Gustavus Adolphus in St. Peter. It is famous for its annual Christmas in Christ Celebration, held in the latter part of November and early December.

One radio station in the Twin Cities, WLTE-FM 102.9, claims it is the official Christmas music station. It plays all Christmas music 24/7 starting before Thanksgiving through December 25. It even has commercial-free segments of 25 songs in a row without commercials. The music sure puts you in a Christmas mood. The station does a good job of mixing in the traditional pieces. This is a sampling of their play list:

- "White Christmas"—Bing Crosby
- "The Christmas Song"—Nat King Cole
- "Rudolph the Red Nosed Reindeer"—Gene Autry
- "All I Want for Christmas Is You"—Mariah Carey
- "Noel"—Josh Groban
- "A Wonderful Christmas Time"—Paul McCartney
- "Hey Santa"—Carmie and Wendy Wilson
- "I Want To Wish You A Merry Christmas"—Jose Feliciano
- "The Christmas Shoes"—Newsong
- "Grandma Got Run Over By a Reindeer"—Dr. Elmo

Somehow, Christmas music sounds better in Minnesota. And it sure sets a festive mood for our winter wonderland.

Minneapolis, with its brilliant light displays and Holidazzle Parade, is considered "the brightest Christmas City" in the nation.

Minnetonka's Icy Plunge
"Fun! Like crashing through a plate glass window"

Minnesota, utilizing its frozen lakes, holds an annual Lake Minnetonka Ice Water Plunge to celebrate the New Year. What does it feel like jumping into a sometimes minus-one-degree air temperature icy lake? One participant, still shaking off the chills after her first dip in the icy waters, put it best: "It's a little like crashing through a plate glass window!"

The Active Life and Running Club (ALARC) sponsor the event each New Year's Day at the Bay View Event Center in Excelsior, just 20 minutes west of Minneapolis. Bill Wenmark, spokesperson for the health group, said there were more than 800 participants in the annual 2008 "On It & In It Lake Minnetonka Ice Plunge." This is a new record for the most people to jump into a frozen lake at one event.

Snowmobilers at Voyageurs National Park. (Photo courtesy Alan Burchell)

Minnesota Picnics
A Sunday tradition for many folks

A joke we used to tell when outsiders would ask what we did in the summertime in Minnesota: "Well," we would tell them, "if it fell on the Fourth of July, we'd go on a picnic." Minnesotans know how to pack a picnic. (And tell a good joke.)

Nearly every Sunday my mother would fill a picnic basket of good eats. Often, we never left the backyard. We had a picnic table beside a shady oak tree that saw lots of use over the years.

— *Author's highlights*

Favorite picnic fixings:

- Hot dogs, hamburgers, and fried chicken
- Ham salad sandwiches
- Baked beans
- German potato salad
- Pickles, stuffed olives, and relish
- Veggie and fruit appetizers
- Watermelon
- Deviled eggs
- Waldorf salad (with marshmallows)
- Marble cake, apple and cherry pie
- Lemonade, iced tea, cold pop, beer, and hot coffee

*S*ome people in New York make fun of our Waldorf salad. Apparently, Minnesotans are the only ones who add marshmallows.

Nature and Vacation Photo Tips
Capture the wonders of Minnesota in your camera

Photography is one hobby in which you can continually learn and improve. I use a Sony Cybershot H9 digital camera that cost about $400. It is fun to experience those special moments when you just instantly say, "Wow!" So far I have recorded about 70 species of birds, 18 different butterflies, and several four-legged critters (deer, skunk, raccoon, chipmunk, squirrel, otter, woodchuck, muskrat, rabbit, and mole). I feel I can always get a better photo the next time. This attitude keeps me alert and aware of my environment, making my surroundings continually interesting.

—Kathy Scott Lampi
The Photo Lady
Grand Rapids

Minnesota's four seasons offer a full spectrum of opportunities as Kathy Scott Lampi, The Photo Lady, illustrates in her cache of pictures.

Kathy Scott Lampi's photo tips and techniques:

1. **Use a digital camera with a zoom lens.** A 10x zoom power or more allows you to get as close as possible without scaring the birds, butterflies, and other critters. Be sure to carry your camera with you, always. Learn what new digital cameras can do.
2. **Take photos all year round.** It will always be a good time to hunt for that right moment to capture a breathtaking landscape, or be surprised by the wildlife. Contrast is important in photography and you will become more aware and appreciative of the wonders of seasonal changes. The snow landscape can be just as interesting as the colors of autumn and as refreshing as the bright colors of spring and summer.

    Many birds migrate to warmer places and other animals hibernate during the winter. However, you still have many choices: Blue jays, cardinals, chickadees, nuthatches, eagles, pigeons, crows, squirrels, rabbits, deer, and sometimes finches.

    You can photograph larger birds and wildlife through glass windows and doors from inside the house no matter what the temperature is outside. Have your zoom lens camera within reach and ready to use even while you read the morning newspaper and drink your cup of coffee or tea.

The Photo Lady . . . Kathy Scott Lampi. (Photo courtesy Kathy Scott Lampi)

3. **Take photos early in the morning or late afternoon,** when the sunlight is softer. Avoid midday, when the sun is directly above you. The light is harsher and more reflective, giving you less contrast.
4. **Capture some action,** such as an adult robin feeding her baby. It is exciting to take a photo of a loon, eagle, or hawk in flight. Action also is good when photographing people. Have your subjects doing something.
5. **Experiment with taking multiple photos from low, medium, and high angles.** Take a profile of the subject. Try to capture the eye of the subject; focusing on that will bring out the personality of the animal.
6. **Provide shelter (a sanctuary) and food to attract wildlife.** Use several feeding stations with seeds, nectar, fruit, grape jelly (for orioles), and water. Birds prefer to land on a nearby branch to look over their territory, since their instincts

are always on guard for danger. Once it appears safe, they go in to feed. Larger birds, like the extremely shy pileated woodpecker, need a large log for their feet and claws, so be sure to provide a log drilled with holes to fill up with suet.

Kathy uses large, trimmed tree limbs propped in an umbrella stand near her bird feeders. She also uses smaller branches for perches in the hanging seed feeders.

You can plant additional evergreen and fruit-bearing trees along with flowers in your yard. Butterflies need flowers to land on. They like Zinnias, daisies, coneflowers, and sedum. In addition, provide sunflowers for the bumblebees and honey bees.

7. **Be patient.** Birds, butterflies, and other animals are extremely aware of your movement because of their excellent eyesight. Sit or stand still, and wait for them to come closer before tak-

ing any pictures. Relax. Let the wildlife become acquainted with you, trusting that you will not do them harm.

8. **Keep a journal to record the wildlife.** Keep on hand guidebooks for birds, butterflies, and animals so you can quickly identify them. This is a great opportunity to learn more about their size, sounds, food preferences, and nesting habits.

9. **Join clubs that sponsor bird watching, nature walks, or photography lessons.** Try finding them through your community-education center or bird-feed store. You may want to start your own nature/photography club. Do not forget to visit your public library. There are many books available for photography, landscaping in Minnesota, and guidebooks for building birdhouses. Subscribe to magazines such as *Popular Photography*.

10. **Share your prize photos.** Print them as postcards, greeting and holiday cards, and be sure you give yourself credit by printing the subject and your name on the back. Family and friends will treasure these cards. Matte and frame a print for a special gift. Enter your best photos at your county fair, or display at your local art gallery.

County Fairs
Not just a preview to the Minnesota State Fair

> When we were teenagers, my sister, Hazel, and I joined the 4-H Club. Mr. Art Frick, the county extension service agent, enrolled us. Through the 4-H we learned to can and pickle what we grew. Then we were encouraged to enter our best results at the Itasca County Fair in Grand Rapids. We did. And we won. We picked up several blue ribbons (for our beets and cucumbers). For us, it was like winning the sweepstakes. Those 4-H days were a rewarding experience for Hazel and me. We attended meetings and met other kids interested in farming. It also taught us that life, as in agriculture, requires planting and cultivating before you can harvest or reap any benefits.
>
> —Remembering Rosy,
> *Esther Johnson Connell*

Nowhere else will you find more local flavor. County fairs have a rich history and have something for everyone. Minnesota 4-H members live for them, excited to display their calves and the crops they cared for all summer, and hopefully, to win a blue ribbon. Local townspeople dust off their favorite cake or pie recipes or get out that quilting masterpiece they made last winter, also hoping to win one of those blue ribbons.

The Minnesota Federation of County Fairs represents 95 fairs throughout the state. The mission of the Minnesota Federation of County Fairs focuses on agriculture and educational opportunities, developing strategies and techniques to advance the fair and special events industry. Moreover, they have been passing along what works at the county level, to the people running the big one—the Minnesota State Fair for decades.

In a way, county fairs are the laboratories for the Minnesota State Fair. County fair managers make up part of the State Fair's board of directors. Their input helps assure building a strong exposition for the state. After all, they are on the firing line throughout the state and know what people want in a fair.

The Itasca County Fair has a beautiful setting, right on the edge of Ice Lake and surrounded by pine trees. It has something for every family. Including fun rides, food stands, 4-H animal barns, machinery exhibit, education booths, and creative activities. It amounts to a miniature state fair and boasts an attendance of 45,000, as Grand Rapids is a major trade area for the Iron Range. It brings in its neighbors from Bemidji, Hibbing, Deer River, Bovey, Aitkin, Cohasset, and a dozen or so more towns in the area.

Many of the county fairs are held in July and early August. See if there is one near you:

- Aitkin County Fair (Aitkin)
- Anoka County Fair (Anoka)
- Becker County Fair (Detroit Lakes)
- Beltrami County Fair (Bemidji)
- Benton County Fair (Sauk Rapids)
- Big Stone County Fair (Clinton)
- Blue Earth County Fair (Garden City)
- Brown County Fair (New Ulm)
- Cannon Valley Fair (Cannon Falls)
- Carlton County Fair (Barnum)
- Carver County Fair (Waconia)
- Cass County Fair (Pillager and Pine River)

- Chippewa County Fair (Montevideo)
- Chisago County Fair (Rush City)
- Clay County Fair (Barnesville)
- Clearwater County Fair (Bagley)
- Cook County Fair (Grand Marais)
- Cottonwood County Fair (Windom)
- Crow Wing County Fair (Brainerd)
- Dakota County Fair (Farmington)
- Dodge County Fair (Kasson)
- Douglas County Fair (Alexandria)
- Faribault County Fair (Blue Earth)
- Fillmore County Fair (Preston)
- Freeborn County Fair (Albert Lea)
- Goodhue County Fair (Zumbrota)
- Grant County Fair (Herman)
- Hennepin County Fair (Corcoran)
- Houston County Fair (Caledonia)
- Hubbard County Fair (Park Rapids)
- Isanti County Fair (Cambridge)
- Itasca County Fair (Grand Rapids)
- Jackson County Fair (Jackson)
- Kanabec County Fair (Mora)
- Kandiyohi County Fair (Willmar)
- Kittson County Fair (Hallock)
- Koochiching County Fair (Northome)
- Lac Qui Parle County Fair (Madison)
- Lake County Fair (Two Harbors)
- Lake of the Woods County Fair (Baudette)
- Le Sueur County Fair (Le Center)
- Lincoln County Fair (Tyler)
- Lyon County Fair (Marshall)

- Mahnomen County Fair (Mahnomen)
- Marshall County Fair (Warren)
- Martin County Fair (Fairmont)
- McLeod County Fair (Hutchinson)
- Meeker County Fair (Litchfield)
- Mille Lacs County Fair (Princeton)
- Morrison County Fair (Motley)
- Morrison County Fair (Little Falls)
- Mower County Fair (Austin)
- Murray County Fair (Slayton)
- Nicollet County Fair (St. Peter)
- Nobles County Fair (Worthington)
- Norman County Fair (Ada)
- Northern Minnesota District Fair (Littlefork)
- Olmsted County Fair (Rochester)
- Ottertail County Fair West (Fergus Falls)
- Ottertail County Fair East (Perham)
- Pennington County Fair (Thief River Falls)
- Pine County Fair (Pine City)
- Pipestone County Fair (Pipestone)
- Polk County Fair (Fertile)
- Pope County Fair (Glenwood)
- Ramsey County Fair (Maplewood)
- Red Lake County Fair (Oklee)
- Redwood County Fair (Redwood Falls)
- Renville County Fair (Bird Island)
- Rice County Fair (Faribault)
- Rock County Fair (Luverne)
- Roseau County Fair (Roseau)
- Scott County Fair (Jordan)
- Sherburne County Fair (Elk River)

- Sibley County Fair (Arlington)
- St. Louis County Fair (Chisholm)
- South St. Louis County Fair (Proctor)
- S.W. St. Louis County Fair (Floodwood)
- Stearns County Fair (Sauk Centre)
- Steele County Free Fair (Owatonna)
- Stevens County Fair (Morris)
- Swift County Fair (Appleton)
- Todd County Fair (Long Prairie)
- Traverse County Fair (Wheaton)
- Tri-County Fair (Mankato)
- Wabasha County Fair (Wabasha)
- Wadena County Fair (Wadena)
- Waseca County Fair (Waseca)
- Washington County Fair (Lake Elmo)
- Watonwan County Fair (St. James)
- Wilkin County Fair (Breckenridge)
- Winona County Fair (St. Charles)
- Wright County Fair (Howard Lake)
- Yellow Medicine County Fair (Canby)

THE
FOUR SEASONS
R E S O R T
On Lake Winnibigoshish

Minnesota State Fair
The Great Minnesota Get-Together

> I first became acquainted with the fair in 1940 as a kid of 10. My brother Kenny, 13, knew how to get us there on the streetcar. He knew all about transferring and everything. There was no worry about where to get off, as the ride terminated at the fairgrounds on Como Avenue. We each had one dollar in our pockets. To make it last, we did a lot of window-shopping. As fairgoers know, there is a lot to see, all free. Then it was time for the rides at the midway. The Ferris wheel was a great bargain—only a dime. The aroma of food was all around us. The hot dog stand pulled us in. Then to wash it down, we went across the street to the milk booth. You could drink as much as you wanted for ten cents. (Today, nearly 20,000 gallons of milk are consumed at $1 for an all-you-can-drink cup.)
>
> — *Author's highlights*

Minnesota State Fair is all Minnesota showcasing our finest agriculture, art, and industry. The Great Minnesota Get-Together offers Twelve Days of Fun ending Labor Day. Started in 1859, it is one of the world's largest, most-visited expositions with an annual attendance over one million people. The fair is successful because it truly reflects the popular culture and concerns of the day. And it is a good way to enjoy a last hurrah before winter sets in. The 320-acre fairground is located at 1265 North Snelling Avenue in St. Paul (651-288-4400, www.mnstatefair.org).

Different people go to our state fair for different reasons. Many go for the midway; Machinery Hill; creative activities including the

The ever popular Midway. (Photo courtesy Minnesota State Fair)

finest needlework, handcrafts, baking, and canning that Minnesota has to offer; the Dairy Building to see the butter sculpture of Princess Kay of the Milky Way; the English or Western Horse shows; the 4-H Animal Barn; the CHS Miracle of Birth Center; the round Horticulture Building with all those eye-catching apples, squash, vegetables, and flowers; the Arts Center; or big-name entertainment at the Grandstand.

And many go to taste what is new on a stick. Concessions feature over 50 foods on a stick including alligator sausage, cheese, vegetable kabobs, walleye, chocolate covered bananas, pickles, pork chops, and Pronto Pups.

For decades, Machinery Hill was a driving force at the fair, displaying at its peak the newest models and products of 13 major tractor companies, plus dozens of short-line firms. Most farmers headed first to Machinery Hill to see the new technology and products that would make their farms more productive. Then in the 1980s, Minnesota farms started to decline. And so did the tractor companies. Mergers took place and reduced the majors to four. And farm equipment dealers began to fade, also. At one time, there were 15,000 John Deere dealers nationally. Today, there are fewer than 1,500. Now, with the agriculture market stabilized, Machinery Hill is still viable and popular at the fair. And as always, many of the city people like to get a peek at what is new in agricultural technology. The kids love to sit in those huge John Deere four-wheel-drive tractors. And so do their dads.

The Minnesota State Fair Grandstand has been booking top entertainers since 1962 when Dennis Day, Jane Russell, and Jimmie Dean headlined. Over 441 music and comedy acts have been enjoyed including The Supremes, Hank Williams, Johnny Cash, Petula Clark, Neil Diamond, Sonny and Cher, Rich Little, Bob Hope, Redd Foxx, Olivia Newton-John, Linda Ronstadt, Bill Cosby, Dolly Parton, KC and the Sunshine Band, The Beach Boys, Rod Stewart, The Oak Ridge Boys, Tom Jones, Garrison Keillor, Peter, Paul and Mary, Jay Leno, Randy Travis, The Simpsons, Garth Brooks, Barry Manilow, B.B. King, Etta James, Vince Gill, ZZ Top, Wynonna, Def Leppard, Ringo Starr, Alicia Keyes, Hootie and the Blowfish, Cyndi Lauper, Clay Aiken, Motley Crue, Amy Grant, "Weird Al" Yankovic, and Fergie.

Country singer/songwriter Willie Nelson starred at The Grandstand 10 times since 1979. In 1982, he asked the show manager to be paid in cash, rather than a check. It took some doing, as Willie was star billing at the Grandstand and was getting big bucks. But the cash was finally rounded up to pay Willie Nelson and his back-up band. His big hit at the time was "On the Road Again." Maybe Willie thought the cash would not leave a paper trail as a check would. However, something the country singer did not know: The state fair was obligated to file a W-9 tax form with the IRS that showed the amount of money he made that year at the Minnesota State Fair. Sorry, Willie.

The Century Farm recognition program began in 1976 to recognize Minnesota farms that have been in continuous ownership by a family for 100 years or more. Over 8,500 Minnesota farms have been designated as a "Century Farm." Recipients receive an outdoor sign and a certificate signed by the governor of Minnesota and presidents of program sponsors, the Minnesota State Fair, and the Minnesota Farm Bureau.

Minnesotans love Willie Nelson. The popular singer has performed at the Minnesota State Fair Grandstand 10 times since 1979. Bet he will be back soon and sing one of his early hits, "On the Road Again."

Minnesota Casinos
Suddenly, flights to Las Vegas were fewer

Casinos brought a new kind of entertainment and excitement to Minnesota. For many, the crowded gaming halls are the perfect destination for a weekend getaway. For others with less time, it is a few hours of diversion from everyday worries. And in the back of the mind of most gamblers, "Maybe today is my lucky day."

Gaming is big business. The state's 18 casinos are a boon with the million-dollar agreements payable to the state. In addition, thousands of people enjoy full-time employment contributing to state taxes. And casinos bring in big-name talent that we might otherwise have gone to Las Vegas, Nevada, or Branson, Missouri, to see. This way, we spend the money in Minnesota to see stars like Brenda Lee, Tom Jones, B. J. Thomas, Willie Nelson, Andy Williams, Bob Newhart, and Jay Leno. Additionally, casinos pay the media millions of dollars of each year with their big advertising budgets.

With the exception of Canterbury Park, all Minnesota casinos are located on Native American reservations and run by the tribes under a contract reached with the state. The minimum and maximum payouts are regulated as follows: video poker and video blackjack are 83% to 98%, slot machines are 80% to 95.9%, and keno is 75% to 95%. Each tribe is free to set its machines to pay back anywhere within those limits.

Most Minnesotans gamble responsibly. However the urge to win can be overpowering, so be careful. Some players lose all sense of reality and stay longer than they should; or worse, bet the farm. Fortunately, all casinos display Gamblers Anonymous and support group information prominently.

Note how the state's casinos are scattered throughout Minnesota.

- Canterbury Park Racetrack and Card Club—Shakopee
- Black Bear Casino & Hotel—Carlton
- Fond-du-Luth Casino—Duluth
- Fortune Bay Resort-Casino—Tower
- Grand Casino Hinckley—Hinckley
- Grand Casino Mille Lacs—Onamia
- Grand Portage Lodge & Casino—Grand Portage
- Jackpot Junction Casino Hotel—Morton
- Little Six Casino—Prior Lake
- Mystic Lake Casino Hotel—Prior Lake
- Northern Lights Casino—Walker
- Palace Casino Hotel—Cass Lake
- Prairie's Edge Casino Resort—Granite Falls
- Seven Clans Casino Hotel & Water Park—Thief River Falls
- Seven Clans Casino Warroad—Warroad
- Shooting Star Casino Hotel—Mahnomen
- Treasure Island Resort Casino—Welch
- White Oak Casino—Deer River

Bowen Lodge guests, Deer River, bring their cameras during the bald eagle viewing activity held on a pontoon. The lodge—on lakes Cut Foot Sioux and Winnibigoshish—boasts the largest breeding population of bald eagles in the lower 48 states.

Chapter Five
Minnesota Legends

Weather Watch
Our record keepers only report the news

Coldest day—February 2, 1993. The tiny town of Tower, in northeast Minnesota, officially recorded an air temperature of **minus 60 degrees F**. Governor Arne Carlson closed all schools in the state that same day. It was only 32 degrees below zero in the Twin Cities.

Hottest day—July 6, 1936. Moorhead reached **114 degrees F**. The summer was hot all over the state. For relief from unbearable days of 100-degree heat, many families slept in parks, trying to catch a breeze. Minneapolis police patrolled the areas for protection.

Most rain—July 23 & 24, 1987. A record-setting seven to eight inches of rain fell in four hours. Some Twin Cities suburbs reported **12 to 14 inches** total for the two-day "rainstorm of the century." Flooding turned the Twin Cities into a huge wading pool and closed major freeways. The most consecutive days of rain record was 10 days experienced in 1951. The longest dry spell was 79 days ending November 9, 1943.

Most snow—October 31, 1991. Twenty-four inches of snow fell in Minneapolis during the Halloween Blizzard of '91. Duluth recorded **36.9 inches**. Duluth also holds the record for earliest recorded snowfall, August 31, 1949. The latest recorded snowfall was in Mizpah on June 4, 1935.

WCCO 8-3-0 Radio
Like a greeter, the Station guides visitors to Minnesota

Through the years, WCCO, Minneapolis/St. Paul, has been as much a part of the community as the 10,000 Lakes, or as The Mall of America. WCCO Radio serves as a greeter for Minnesota. Like a welcoming beacon, the station helps guide visitors from as far away as Colorado. Closer by, WCCO is no stranger to the folks from the bordering states and Canada. Many have pulled in the strong 8-3-0 signal and gotten acquainted with our market along the way. Drivers and their passengers keep tuned to the station to catch up on the news, weather, sports, local conditions—and gossip, on their journey from Wisconsin, Iowa, North Dakota, or South Dakota to our vacationland. Then upon reaching their destination—be it a northern resort, relatives, friends, or a shopping spree to the great MOA—they feel more relaxed and better prepared for their visit.

Akin to "That Ol' Man River," the broadcaster has been rolling along on its giant 50,000-watt clear channel, for 80-plus years. Residents and visitors alike know its slogan *"Minnesota's Good Neighbor,"* by heart and know WCCO talks their language. Anglers, bait shop and resort owners always tune in for one of Minnesota's big events, The Governor's Fishing Opener. From its beginning in 1948, the May opener celebrates the kickoff for the walleye fishing season and the start of the summer tourism season. In Minnesota, that is big news. That is why WCCO announcers are just a boat away—when Governors Arne Carlson, Jesse Ventura, or Tim Pawlenty—take their turns casting for "the big one." WCCO built a good corps of stringers to call in the latest catches from lakes all across the region. Like the report from Lake Winnibigoshish in 1957 with a record muskie, catch of 54 pounds. (That is big news, too, and no fish story.) The record catch, as reported on WCCO, spread around the region

A proud young lady with her prize northern pike at Voyageurs National Park.
(Photo courtesy Alan Burchell)

like wildfire. And just as sure as Winnie is one of the hot spots for fishing, you can be sure WCCO Radio will update the story when someone sets a new record. Maybe it will be you.

Voices that have signed-off from WCCO include the following:

- **Cedric Adams**—His warm, deep, authoritative voice, with an infectious laugh, made him the most popular air personality in the region. After signing off his 10 O'clock Taystee Bread newscast the Twin Cities would go dark. His dual media role as both news columnist and broadcaster made him one of Minnesota's most popular personalities.

- **Boone & Erickson**—You could always expect the unexpected when Charlie Boone and Roger Erickson were on the air. Contrast helped make Boone and Erickson one of the team legends of American radio. Boone & Erickson attracted many loyal sponsors that they became closely identified with over their 25 years together. Charlie Boone can still be heard on Saturday mornings on WCCO. He also records for "Talking Books Radio" books for the blind.

- **Clellan Card**—Card was one of the top talents in the 1940s. He was an announcer, actor, comedian, and master of ceremonies. His *Quiz of the Twin Cities*, with Bob DeHaven, achieved high ratings. Card switched to WCCO TV as Axel Torgeson on *Axel and His Dog*, a popular children's program. Grownups also loved the show, maybe because of Carmen the Nurse played by Mary Davies.

- **Joyce Lamont**—Known as the "recipe lady" she hosted programs featuring travel, community events, and cooking for over 40 years at WCCO. Joyce was the Twin Cities' first female announcer. Many listeners thought she was broadcasting from her kitchen. She would carefully repeat each ingredient so every listener would get the recipe right. Her folksy manner for giving a recipe like pineapple upside-down cake generated monthly fan mail of 10,000 letters. She hosted a morning show on KLBB in Minneapolis after leaving WCCO in 1989 and retired from radio in 2003.

- **Burt Hanson**—Burt's inspiring voice entertained listeners for decades. Jack Benny had his tenor, Dennis Day, but WCCO had Burt Hanson. He and Ramona Gerhard, organist for the station, had their own record label, Mona. Their best-selling disk included "Because" and "My God and I." Where have all the tenors gone?

- **Howard Viken**—The quintessential announcer was unaffected by all the glamour around him. Howard performed for nearly 40 years at the station and won new fans each day. He just started at KDAL, Duluth, in 1950 when WCCO hired him away. He helped put Bob Newhart on the map by playing his "Driving Instructor" episode from *The Button-Down Mind of Bob Newhart* album. He did the same for the Weavers/Gordon Jenkins *Good Night Irene* record. (And no payola.)

- **Harry Reasoner**—Harry started as a news writer at WCCO Radio and then moved in front of the camera as a news anchor on KMSP TV, Channel 9. His next stop was CBS in New York. He made news when he and Barbara Walters became the first male/female co-anchors on ABC TV. The University of Minnesota awarded an honorary diploma to Reasoner for his real-life experiences. (He attended the school for three years, but never graduated.)

When asked where he would like to vacation in Minnesota, a small boy from Iowa replied: "Anywhere close to Paul Bunyan." A legend so big, Paul Bunyan is found in numerous towns, including Akeley, Bemidji, Brainerd, and Chisholm.

Minnesota Mile Markers
Events and technologies that changed our lives

> Long before scrolling for weather on cell phones or portable electronic devices, my generation received forecasts from a huge ball. We all knew how to read it: "White: cold in sight; red: warmer weather ahead; green: no change foreseen; blinking: precipitation's on the way." At night, the ball could be seen from 15 miles away! The Northwestern Bank Weather Ball inaugural lighting, on the Minneapolis bank's roof at Sixth and Marquette, was broadcasted by WCCO Radio. Other parts of the nation may have thought it was no big deal, but for Minnesota in 1949, it was a major event. As a Page Boy at WCCO, I was up there helping Bob DeHaven, master of ceremonies, producers, engineers, the mayor, and other dignitaries put the show on. The Weather Ball stood tall in the eyes of all weather-minded Minnesotans, which was everyone.
>
> — *Author's highlights*

- **Interstate Highway 35W Bridge Collapse**—Emergency responders, survivors, and passersby worked heroically to provide rescue and medical aid to victims when the bridge in downtown Minneapolis collapsed and fell into the Mississippi River during rush hour on August 1, 2007. The 13 deaths and 100 injuries raised bridge-safety consciousness across the United States. Our 911 emergency service employees received a national award for their outstanding work in handling the thousands of desperate calls. Government agencies, charities, local corporations, and volunteers provided assistance and donations. Minutes after the media filed the first stories about the I-35W collapse the long-distance calls reached many cell phones: "Are you okay?" "Were you on it?" "What can we do to help?" We were quickly reminded that everyone cares about Minnesota. The compassion the nation showed our state was heartwarming. The Minnesota Department of Transportation is planning a replacement bridge, to be called the St. Anthony Falls 35W Bridge. Meanwhile, thousands of riders are taking alternate routes, and not complaining.

- **Light Rail**—Hop aboard! The Metro Transit Hiawatha Line opened in 2004 and offers fast, quiet light-rail service to 17 stations between downtown Minneapolis and the Mall of America. Some of the stops include Lake Street/Midtown, the VA Medical Center, Fort Snelling, and the Minneapolis/St. Paul International Airport. Not up to full speed with riders, yet. Metro Transit, a service of the Metropolitan Council, knows more people would use it if they tried it. In addition, it is a neat way for tourists to see Minneapolis. Planners are considering a light rail running from St. Cloud to the Twin Cities that would open up the metro's western corridor, and another connecting downtown Minneapolis with downtown St. Paul.

- **Super Bowl XXVI**—The Humphrey Metrodome hosted its first Super Bowl on January 26, 1992, but without the Minnesota Vikings. At first, the Super Bowl committee thought Minneapolis might be too cold in January, but the skyway system helped change their minds. After all, we are known as the "Skyway Capital of America." The interconnected and sometimes heated walkways between downtown buildings were filled during Super Bowl XXVI with the thousands of visitors. The Washington Redskins (NFC) beat the Buffalo Bills (AFC) with a final score of 37-24.

- **Minnesota Casinos**—The day Mystic Lake opened in 1992 was a day that people from our neighboring borders—Canada, North Dakota, South Dakota, Iowa, and Wisconsin—came to play indoors. This is not to overlook the thousands from the Twin Cities area and outstate Minnesota that also stopped by. Suddenly we became one of the "fun states." Visitors could not believe their eyes when they saw the Mystic Lake Casino, owned and operated by the Shakopee Mdewakanton Sioux Community, in Prior Lake. They thought they were in Las Vegas. The 18 Native American casinos located all over the state and operated by 11 tribes have added a new form of entertainment for Minnesotans and our region since the federal Indian Gaming Regulatory Act, passed in 1988 to promote tribal economies.
- **The Halloween Blizzard of 1991**—24 inches in 24 hours—was the largest snowfall from a single storm in Minnesota history. Duluth was buried with over three feet of snow early on October 31. The three-day storm was the longest lasting on record. It was also very hard on wildlife. Schools, businesses, and roads were closed for days. The early snowfall made for a long winter that year.
- **World Series Champions**—Winning baseball's World Series the first time, in 1987, made Minnesota Twins fans a little crazy. The second time, four years later, we went wild! ESPN called the 1991 World Series the best ever. The Twins beat the Atlanta Braves in seven games. Jack Morris, the winning pitcher, was the MVP. Seven players were in both series: Kirby Puckett, Kent Hrbeck, Greg Gagne, Dan Gladden, Randy Bush, Gene Larken, and Al Newman. And of

course, so was Tom Kelly, the winning coach. The Twins stadium announcer, Bob Casey, became famous with his introduction "and here's number 34, K I R B Y P U C K E T!"

- **Blizzard of the 20**TH **Century**—November 11, 1940, Armistice Day (now Veteran's Day). Minneapolis had 16 inches of snowfall that day. Collegeville recorded 27 inches. Rural Minnesota experienced 20-foot-high drifts. Hundreds of duck hunters were trapped by the storm sometimes referred to as "the winds of hell" with gusts reaching 50 to 80 miles per hour. They found themselves in a life-and-death struggle. Forty-nine people died in Minnesota; 150 nationwide. There was no warning that the Armistice Day Blizzard was on the way. Very few of the hunters carried a winter survival kit, as Minnesotans are now urged to do. To improve early storm warnings weather forecasting was expanded, at Minnesota's governor's and congressman's urging, to 24-hour coverage from additional weather offices.

Best Books
Minnesota's amazing literary landscape

"Books are the best value for your time and money." That is what Mrs. Whiting, my English teacher, used to tell our eighth-grade class. I first acquired my reading habit as a young boy at the Franklin Avenue Library, Thirteenth and Franklin in Minneapolis. To own a library card made me feel important and responsible because my mother made sure the material was returned on time.

— *Author's highlights*

Minnesota's authors, poets, playwrights, storytellers, essayists, and humorists have expanded the world for thousands of readers. Their creative talent is recognized with winners of the Pulitzer Prize, National Book Award, Nobel Prize in Literature (Sinclair Lewis was the first American awarded the prize), Newbery medal, Caldecott medal, and Minnesota Book Award.

Whenever possible, try to support Minnesota authors by requesting their books from your local library or purchasing them from an independent bookseller, retail chain, or web-based site.

The Minnesota Historical Society, Metronet, and the Minnesota Center for the Book are working together to produce the Minnesota Author Biographies Project. Currently the database contains biographies for 36 authors. A bibliography of significant works is included for each Minnesota author. Also links to additional resources in print and on-line (www. people.mnhs.org/authors).

According to "America's Most Literate Cities" survey, Minneapolis has been in the top 10 rankings every year and St. Paul has been in the top 10 for the past four years moving up to third in 2007.

These past and present authors were born in Minnesota, are currently residing here, or lived here previously. A few are listed in the Minnesota Biographies Project. Many more will follow. Listed alphabetical by author:

- *Shelter Half*, by Carol Bly (Duluth)
- *Iron John*, by Robert Bly (Madison)
- *My Family is Forever*, by Nancy Carlson (Edina)
- *Remembering Rosy*, by Esther Johnson Connell (Itasca County)
- *The Tale of Despereaux*, by Kate DiCamillo (Minneapolis)

- *Tender Is the Night,* by Francis Scott Fitzgerald (St. Paul)
- *Ordinary People,* by Judith Guest (Edina)
- *North of Hope,* by Jon Hassler (Minneapolis, also lived in Staples and Plainview)
- *A Cup of Christmas Tea,* by Thomas Hegg (Eden Prairie), illustrated by Warren Hanson (St. Paul)
- *Mr. Roberts,* by Thomas Heggen (Minneapolis)
- *Lake Wobegon Days,* by Garrison Keillor (Anoka)
- *Main Street,* by Sinclair Lewis (Sauk Centre)
- *Betsy-Tacy,* by Maud Hart Lovelace (Mankato)
- *Mike Lynch's Minnesota Weatherwatch,* by Mike Lynch
- *Morte d'Urabn,* by J.F. Powers (Collegeville)
- *Officer Buckle and Gloria,* by Peggy Rathmann (St. Paul, also lived in New Brighton)
- *Take the Cold Out of Cold Calling* (Web Search Secrets), by Sam Richter (Minnetonka)
- *Minnesota North Stars* (History and Memories with Lou Nanne), by Bob Showers (Bloomington)
- *Little House On the Prairie,* by Laura Ingalls Wilder (Walnut Grove and Spring Valley)

Many families have a tradition of reading Tom Hegg's **A Cup of Christmas Tea** *every holiday. Tom is a Master Teacher at Breck School in Golden Valley.*

Remembering Minnesota
by Betty Kilby Hensley, San Diego

My Minnesota memories go back to 1935 when the lack of jobs in Duluth moved us to a wide place in the road called Silverdale, in the southeastern corner of Koochiching County. It is near the communities of Rauch and Greaney. We went from a home with a stoker furnace, indoor plumbing, and running water to an old farmhouse on several acres with no water. Like pioneers in the wilderness, it was adventuresome finding, chopping, splitting, and carrying the wood to feed the kitchen stove and a barrel stove in the living room. We carried our water from a pool half a mile away. I have returned for the community's Greaney Rauch Silverdale History Day Picnic and became reacquainted with cousins and neighbors I had not seen for 60 years. I am proud of the area's heritage: people from Norway, Sweden, Finland, Russia, Austria, Hungary, Italy, Yugoslavia, and Poland. My wonderful Minnesota memories came flowing back when we visited at the GRS Community Center.

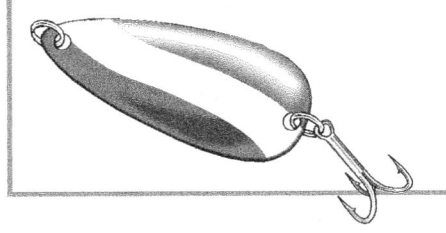

Minnesota Celebrities
From superstars to Superman

My Minnesota memories are many. After graduating from North High School in 1950, I attended the University of Minnesota and worked at WCCO Radio as a page boy. Working with the best in broadcast, I learned plenty. Harry Reasoner, a newsman writing Cedric Adams' newscasts, taught me the "Rip and Read" theory: how to sight-read and be ready for live broadcasting. It helped me enormously in Hollywood during readings and auditions for movie and TV roles. I had the early-morning shift and kept Roger Krupp, a former CBS network announcer, loaded with hot coffee before his announcing duties. Bob DeHaven used to kid me about dressing better than he did. (I always loved clothes.) I got in hot water once with Jack Lucas, boss of the page boys. He assigned me to deliver the 10 p.m. news copy to Cedric Adams' home in Edina for a remote broadcast. Only problem was I had trouble driving the '41 Cadillac limousine—and got lost. After that, I believe the policy was to have a backup copy at the station. I return to Minnesota as often as I can.

—Robert Vaughn, movie and TV actor,
Ridgefield, Connecticut

Remarks: Good news for Minnesota author book lovers and *The Man from U.N.C.L.E* fans. Robert Francis Vaughn has just written his autobiography, *A Fortunate Life*. Vaughn lived in Minneapolis while a high school student and college freshman studying journalism.

- **Eddie Albert** (1906–2005). Born Edward Albert Heimberger. His family moved to Minneapolis in 1907. A graduate of Minneapolis Central High School and the University of Minnesota, he left his mark on Broadway in 100 films and television. He was a hit as the traveling salesman in *Oklahoma*. Albert may be best remembered for *Green Acres* on TV. He was a lieutenant in the U.S. Coast Guard, served in the Pacific during WWII, and awarded a Bronze Star medal for heroism. Albert was married twice and had two children. He was a special envoy for Meals for Millions in 1963 and helped launch Earth Day.
- **Arlene Dahl** was born in Minneapolis in 1928. She is a Minneapolis Washburn High School graduate and the mother of three children including actor Lorenzo Lamas. She was a beautiful redhead in MGM Technicolor movies during the post World War II years. She starred in 30 films, but her best film was *Three Little Words* in 1950. She won 10 Laurel Awards for her movies. She has appeared in 19 plays including Broadway's *Applause*. Arlene guest starred on many television series and played in ABC's *One Life to Live* soap opera from 1981–1984. Two of her six husbands were actors Lex Barker and Fernando Lamas. She resumed her film acting in 1991. She received the "Lifetime Achievement Award" in 1994.
- **Bob Dylan**. Born Robert Zimmerman in Hibbing in 1941. Dylan became a folksinger, songwriter, musician, author, and poet. His biggest hit was "Blowin' in the Wind" in 1962, and he set a standard for protest songs. He is in the Rock & Roll Hall of Fame. To help keep his memory alive, Hibbing annually holds a "Bob Dylan Days" festival. A private person, the paparazzi cannot locate the superstar for any new photos. His music has won Grammys, Golden Globes,

and Academy Awards. In April 2008 the Pulitzer Prize committee awarded Dylan with a rare special citation "for his profound impact on popular music and American culture."
- **Judy Garland** (1922–1969). Born Francis Gumm in Grand Rapids to a show business family, she signed an MGM contract at age 13. Judy showed her talents with Mickey Rooney in several musicals: She was awarded a Juvenile Oscar in 1940 for her best movie, *The Wizard of Oz*, featuring her signature song, "Over the Rainbow." During WWII, she regularly performed in USO shows for the stateside armed forces. Her memory and the Land of Oz live on at the Judy Garland Museum in Grand Rapids.
- **Garrison Keillor**. Born Gary Edward Keillor in Anoka in 1942. Writer, storyteller, columnist, radio performer, musician, humorist, and satirist. 1999 National Humanities Medal winner. 1987 Grammy for Best Spoken Word Album. He was inducted into the Radio Hall of Fame in 1994. Keillor graduated from the University of Minnesota, class of 1966. He hosts the Minnesota public radio show, *A Prairie Home Companion,* on Saturday nights. His old-style variety radio show reaches millions of listeners each week. In its twenty-seventh season it is performed before a live audience and broadcast on almost 600 public radio stations including America One and the Armed Forces Networks in Europe and the Far East. Garrison has written 13 books. He gained new fans with his book *Lake Wobegon Days* published in 1985. Garrison's latest book is *Pontoon*. Twice divorced, he married a violinist, Jenny Lind Nilsson, from Anoka, in 1995. One of their homes is in St. Paul. He has two children.
- **Jessica Lange** was born in Cloquet in 1949. She studied art at the University of Minnesota and attended the Guthrie

Theater Drama School. Jessica lived in rural Minnesota for a few years with actor Sam Shepard and their three children. Her first film was *King Kong* in 1976. Her role as Cora in *The Postman Always Rings Twice* (1981) with Jack Nicholson helped make her a star. She won Oscars for her roles in *Blue Sky* (1994) and *Tootsie* (1982). She produced two films: *Cheri* (2008) and *Country* (1984). She debuted on Broadway in *A Streetcar Named Desire*. She is a former United Nations Children's ambassador and is now the ambassador for Save the Children.

- **Charles A. Lindbergh, Jr.** (1902–1974). Aviator, explorer, inventor, writer, and activist, Lindbergh grew up on a farm near Little Falls. He graduated from Little Falls High School in 1918. His father Charles Arthur Lindbergh, Sr., was a U.S. Congressman from Minnesota's sixth district (1907–1917). "Lucky Lindy" achieved the first solo, nonstop flight across the Atlantic to Paris in 1927. *The Spirit of St. Louis* was his airplane and title of his first book. He was awarded the congressional Medal of Honor in 1928 for his courage, navigational skill, and heroic life risking flight. At the time a captain in the Army Air Service Reserve Corps, he was first commissioned in 1925. He and Anne Morrow were married in New Jersey in 1929. Tragically, their son was kidnapped and killed in 1932. He fathered 11 children. The Minneapolis-St. Paul International Airport named its new 1962 passenger terminal Lindbergh Terminal in his honor. The Charles A. Lindbergh, Jr., historic site is located two miles south of Little Falls, on Lindbergh Drive.
- **John Madden** was born in Austin in 1936. Madden is one of the top football analysts around. He wears a Super Bowl ring, which he won as coach of the Oakland Raiders after beating

the Minnesota Vikings 32-14 in 1977. He is a 2006 Pro Football Hall of Fame Inductee. John started The John Madden Hall of Fame Education Foundation to provide transportation to the museum for schools and organizations for economically disadvantaged youth. He still gets in some ice fishing when covering the Vikes. He refuses to fly and has a $100,000-plus bus to go from NFL city to city for *Sunday Night Football*. John also hosts a daily radio show on KCBS.

- **Noel Neill** was born in Minneapolis in 1920. Her father, George, was a Minneapolis newspaper editor. She graduated from Minneapolis Central High School and was an enthusiastic alumna. Noel spoke to the student body frequently and told about her Hollywood connection. Superman fans will remember her as reporter Lois Lane in the original *Superman* TV series in the 1950s. Typecast, she had a hard time getting other decent parts, but did cameos in several films and appeared in two Western serials. She recently appeared in the 2006 motion picture *Superman Returns*. She has been married twice.

- **Prince.** Born Prince Rogers Nelson in 1958 in Minneapolis. Singer, songwriter, musician, composer, record producer, actor, and dancer. Grammy Award winner, Academy Award winner, Golden Globe nominee, and inducted into the Rock and Roll Hall of Fame in 2004. The legendary musician changed the course of popular music. Composing, arranging, performing, and producing almost all of the songs on his albums. His R&B, funk, and soul music became known as the "Minneapolis sound." He won a Grammy in 2008 for Best Male R&B Vocal Performance with *Future Baby Mama*. Prince's best-known movie is *Purple Rain*, which won the 1984 Oscar for Best Original Song Score. His halftime show at the Super Bowl XLI in Miami reached 140 million viewers, his largest audience. Paisley Park, his high-tech recording studio is in Chanhassen. Prince fans have spotted him grocery shopping at Byerly's at midnight in his hometown, and he has attended Minnesota Timberwolves games.

- **Robert Vaughn** was born in 1932 to radio and stage acting parents. When his parents separated, his mother, Marcella, moved with him to Minneapolis. He graduated from North High School, class of 1950. He worked as a WCCO Radio page boy while a college freshman. Hollywood bound, Robert Vaughn won an Academy Award nomination for *The Young Philadelphians* (1959) with Paul Newman. His next big hit was *The Magnificent Seven* (1960). His most memorable role was Napoleon Solo in the TV spy series *The Man from U.N.C.L.E.* He won an Emmy for his role in *Washington: Behind Closed Doors* (1977). He attended the University of Minnesota for just one year before transferring to Los Angeles City College where he majored in drama. He has a master's degree in theater from L.A. State College and a PhD in communications from USC. He married Linda Staab in 1974 and has two children.

Robert Vaughn attended the University of Minnesota and acted on KUOM Radio before Hollywood. (Photo courtesy robertvaughn.com)

All Star Team
Minnesota's greatest athletes

> Every kid needs someone to look up to, and sports heroes are often their first choice. When I was an eight year old, in the Knot Hole Gang, I talked with Ted Williams at Nicollet Park. The future Baseball Hall of Famer was sent to our minor league team the Minneapolis Millers. We met again 15 years later in Korea. He was a Marine jet fighter pilot, and I was a Marine radio correspondent assigned to interview him in 1953. He served two military tours of duty while he played for the Boston Red Sox. Ted married Doris Soule (the first of three wives) in 1944 the same day he was commissioned as a second lieutenant at Pensacola. They met five years earlier in Princeton, Minnesota, where he liked to go fishing. During Ted Williams' 19 seasons as an outfielder, he hit 521 home runs with a .344 lifetime batting average. The Red Sox retired his #9 in 1984.
>
> — *Author's highlights*

The sports world respects Minnesota for its All Americans, Olympic champions, and athletic super stars. *Sports Illustrated* magazine recognized 50 of the greatest twentieth century Minnesota Athletes in their fiftieth anniversary edition. Here is our own historic sampling of sports greats:

- **Jeanne Arth**, St. Paul, tennis player, 1959 Wimbledon Doubles Champion with Darlene Hard

- **Ken Bartholomew,** speed skater, 1948 Olympic Silver Medal Winner, 14 National Championship Titles, 1974 Senior Olympic Gold Medal Winner (4)
- **Charles Albert "Chief" Bender,** White Earth Indian Reservation, pitcher, Baseball Hall of Fame, three World Series Titles, Philadelphia Athletics 1903–17
- **Patty Berg,** Minneapolis, golfer, 1946 U.S. Women's Open Winner, won 57 LPGA events, 29 Amateur Titles
- **Bernie Bierman,** Springfield, coach, University of Minnesota Gophers football head coach 16 seasons, six Big Ten Championships, five National Championships, and five undefeated seasons. Also coached at Montana, Mississippi State, and Tulane
- **Herb Brooks,** St. Paul, hockey player and coach, 1980 Olympic Gold Medal Winner team coach, 1968 and '64 U.S. Olympic hockey team player, coached Minnesota North Stars, International Hockey Hall of Fame
- **Rod Carew,** first baseman, Baseball Hall of Fame 1991, All-Star, seven batting titles, American League MVP award, Minnesota Twins, and the California Angels
- **John Gagliardi,** Collegeville, football coach—51 years. St. John's—47 years. 364 wins (second all time wins)
- **Vern Gagne,** Robbinsdale, wrestler, 1949 and '48 NCAA Wrestling Titles, won Tag-Team Title with Bronko Nakurski, professional wrestler
- **Jean Havlish,** St. Paul, shortstop, All-American Girls Professional Baseball League (AAGPBL), Fort Wayne Daisies 1950, Hall of Fame Bowler
- **Tom Lehman,** Alexandria, golfer, 2000 Phoenix Open Winner, 1999 Ryder Cup Team U.S.A. Winner, 1996 British Open Champion, 1996 Tour Championship Winner, 1995 Colonial

National Invitational Winner, 1994 Memorial Tournament Winner, 1996 PGA Player of the Year
- **John Mariucci**, Eveleth, hockey player and coach, 1956 Olympic Silver Medal Winner Team U.S.A., 18 record wins as Gopher Coach, nicknamed the Godfather of Hockey in Minnesota. NHL Hockey Hall of Fame 1985, U.S. Hockey Hall of Fame 1973, Chicago Black Hawks
- **Kevin McHale**, Hibbing, basketball player, NBA Champion (3), NBA All-Star (7), The Top Player in University of Minnesota Basketball History, Boston Celtics
- **George Mikan**, basketball player, NBL, BAA, and NBA Champion (7), NBA All-Stars (4), All-Star MVP 1953, Greatest Player of the first Half Century, Minneapolis Lakers
- **Bronko Nagurski**, International Falls, football player, All American Tackle 1929 University of Minnesota Football, Chicago Bears Pro Fullback, Professional Football Hall of Fame 1963, World Heavyweight Champion professional wrestler, and UCLA Football Coach
- **Lou Nanne**, Edina, hockey player and coach, Minnesota Gophers Hockey, WCHA MVP 1963, 1968 Olympic Hockey Team U.S.A., International Ice Hockey Federation Hall of Fame and U.S. Hockey Hall of Fame, North Stars Hockey
- **Cindy Nelson**, Lutsen, 1976 Olympic Bronze Medal Winner Alpine Skiing—Downhill, 1982 and 1980 Silver Medal Winner World Championships—Downhill & Combined, six World Cup Wins in Downhill, Giant Slalom & Super-G
- **Amy Peterson**, Maplewood, speedskater, 1994 Olympic Bronze Medal Winner (2) and 1992 Olympic Silver Medal Winner, Speedskating Hall of Fame
- **Kirby Puckett**, center fielder, baseball, 1987 and 1991 World Series Champion, Silver Slugger (6), Golden Glove (6), All-

Star (10), 1993 All-Star MVP, Baseball Hall of Fame 2001, Minnesota Twins
- **John Roethlisberger**, Afton, gymnast, National Gymnastics Titles 1995, '93, '92 and '90, 2000 and 1996 U.S. Olympic team, U of M Gopher Gymnastics
- **Briana Scurry**, Dayton, goalie, soccer, 2004 and 1996 Olympic Gold Medal Winner Team U.S.A. and 1999 World Cup Champion Team U.S.A., a founder of the WUSA, All-State at Anoka High
- **Fran Tarkenton**, quaterback, football, Pro Bowl (9), All Pro (6), 1975 NFL MVP, "The Scrambler," Pro Football Hall of Fame 1986, 18 seasons with the Minnesota Vikings Football and the New York Giants
- **Ted Williams**, baseball player and manager, 1946 A.L. Pennant, Baseball Hall of Fame 1966, 1949, and '46 MVP, six batting titles, All-Star (17), A.L. Triple Crown (2) Major League Player of the Year (5), IGFA Fishing Hall of Fame, Minneapolis Millers, Boston Red Sox, Washington Senators, Texas Rangers

When the Minneapolis Lakers played New York in 1949, the Madison Square Garden marquee read: "Geo. Mikan vs. the Knicks." The 6' 10" Mikan led the Lakers to five NBA titles.

Paul Bunyan and Pals
Minnesota's icons shine worldwide

> I grew up with Paul Bunyan in Bemidji. I miss seeing him and Babe, the blue ox that greeted visitors as they drove into my hometown. I learned about his legend at the Paul Bunyan Museum in Bemidji. Christmas meant going to grandma's house in Mill Park. We always had dinner first: lutefisk, lefse, and all the trimmings. Yummmm. In the summer, I went by train to Grand Rapids and visited cousins. Lots of fun, trees, and lakes. Once we went to the Itasca County Fair, which was wonderful.
>
> —Joan Hagen Raznatovich
> Roseville, California

Minnesota has a reputation for developing lovable icons and mascots.

- **Paul Bunyan** and **Babe the Blue Ox**—Almost every schoolchild learned about the lumberjack's feats: how he and Babe, because they were so big and strong, created Minnesota's 10,000 lakes with their footsteps, including Lake Bemidji. So big is their legend, Paul Bunyan and Babe the Blue Ox can be found in numerous locations, including Akeley, Bemidji, and Brainerd. Just follow the thousands of tourists.
- **The Green Giant** and **Pillsbury Doughboy**—International favorites. The Green Giant brand took off when the *Jolly Green Giant* appeared on packaging and television ads. The Pillsbury icon stands tall in LeSueur, original home of the Minnesota Valley Canning Company. The name was

changed to the Green Giant Company and eventually joined the Pillsbury Company. Another Pillsbury trademark that made quite a name for himself is *Poppin' Fresh, the Pillsbury Doughboy*, who came to life on television via Pillsbury refrigerated products. In the 1970s, a toy *Doughboy* family was created and sold at Sears.

- **Betty Crocker**—Perhaps the prettiest of all corporate icons. The Washburn Crosby Company, later renamed General Mills, invented the character in 1921 to personalize letters in response from customers. By 1936, Betty had become so popular, the company created a face to go along with her signature. In 1950, the first *Betty Crocker* cookbook was published and quickly became a staple in American kitchens. She is a fictional food expert for General Mills, despite many consumers believing she is "real." Just like a real woman, her image has been updated eight times.

Paul Bunyan and Babe the Blue Ox at home adjacent to the Bemidji Tourist Information Center since 1937. (Photo courtesy Visit Bemidji)

- **The Hamm's Bear**—"That funny bear in the TV commercial was better than the program we were watching," commented many TV viewers. That pretty much sums up the popularity of the lovable, animated Hamm's Bear in his long TV run in the 1950s and 1960s. He was television's first icon. The first commercials were black and white using combined animation and live action. Everyone loved him. He was salesman extraordinaire. Besides helping to move truckloads of barrels of Hamm's beer, he also helped promote Minnesota tourism, and more. The breakthrough TV commercials that featured a refreshing lake-country setting, musical tom-toms, and a catchy tag line, *"From the Land of Sky Blue Waters,"* with the bear in the middle of it all, made Minneapolis a major advertising center. A second strong theme came out of the material: "America's most refreshing beer," both lines were used in the ads.

Hamm's locked into the campaign for over 20 years, which is uncommon in advertising. Hamm's beer sales rose from 800,000 barrels in 1946 to 4,311,000 at the contract's end in 1969.

Ray Mithun, co-founder and president of Campbell Mithun, the agency that developed the Hamm's advertising, wrote in a 1969 memo: "We believe the legend of the Hamm's bear, like that of Paul Bunyan, will grow greater and greater as time goes on." Ray, a taskmaster who inspired his team, is in the Advertising Hall of Fame because of creative work that includes the Hamm's campaign.

Books have written about the lovable-bear phenomenon. One was *The Paws of Refreshment: a History of Hamm's Beer*

Advertising, by Moira F. Harris. Marketing classes also relive the history so that younger generations can be exposed to some great advertising. Memorabilia collectors continue their quest for the merchandise items with the bear on it, such as clocks, ashtrays, signs, posters, placemats, glassware, and ceramic miniatures. The items go up in value each day.

In 2000, *The St. Paul Pioneer Press* named the bear as runner-up on its list of "150 Influential Minnesotans of the past 150 years."

The Hamm's Beer TV Bear. (Photo courtesy Campbell Mithun)

Chapter Six
Business Minded

Minnesota Made
Gifted brands with a value-added touch

> Historically Minnesotans have such a good work record that people in human resources tend to favor hiring us nationwide. Innovation, creativity, perseverance, and hard-working employees continue to build many successful Minnesota corporations. Today the "Land of 10,000 Lakes" has over one million businesses and 80,000 manufacturers, according to the Saint Paul Port Authority.
>
> *— Author's highlights*

You contribute to the state's economic well being each time you use a product made in Minnesota, whether travelling or at home. You may not realize how many Minnesota brands subtly touch your daily life. From the food you eat, which may be from General Mills to the food you give your pet, which may be from Cargill. When you open a checking account at Wells Fargo Bank or get your hair cut at a Regis salon. And if you ever need cardiac or other medical implants then Minnesota-based Medtronic or St. Jude Medical may in turn contribute to your physical well being.

Minnesota is home to both publicly and privately owned giants in industry as well as leaders in small business. Companies provide worldwide service in aerospace, agribusiness, broadcasting, communications, energy, food processing, financial services, gaming, health care, leisure, manufacturing, medical devices, retail, technology, printing, and publishing.

We encourage you to use these products selected from companies headquartered here and of course, all the other Minnesota-made, value-added products.

In the Kitchen

- Bake a dozen biscuits *with Bisquick Original Pancake and Baking Mix*
- Toss a salad with *Bushel Boy* tomatoes
- Heat a bowl of *Byerly's Wild Rice Soup* in the microwave
- Eat *Cheerios* for breakfast
- Brush your Minnesota grown corn on the cob with *Land O' Lakes Butter*
- Stick a colorful yellow *Post-it Note* by 3M on the refrigerator
- Eat a slice of deep dish pan-style *Red Baron Pizza*
- Stir *Watkins Pure Vanilla Extract* into your recipes

Around the House or Farm

- Open a window from *Andersen* or *Marvin*
- Energize your hair with *Rosemary Mint Shampoo* from *Aveda*
- Write out a "Wizard of Oz" check printed by *Deluxe Checks*
- Bundle up for warmth with a *Fairbo Woolen Blanket*
- Keep your tractor oiled with *Farm-Oyl Brand Engine Oil*
- Record vacation videos on a DVD from *Imation*
- Play with a puzzle from *LARK Wooden Toys*

- Put some candy in a collectible crock from *Red Wing Stoneware*
- Stock your pantry with *SPAM Golden Honey Grail*
- Spruce up the yard with equipment from the *Toro Company*

Desserts and Dining Out

- Treat yourself to a *Blizzard* of the month at a *Dairy Queen*
- Order the *Silver Butter Knife Steak* for two at *Murray's*
- Snack on a real milk chocolate original *Pearson's Nut Goodie*
- Lick a cone packed with *Sebastian Joe's Ice Cream*
- Enjoy a bucket of chocolate chip cookies from *Sweet Martha's Cookie Jar*

Outdoor and Leisure

- Ride a snowmobile from *Arctic Cat* or *Polaris*
- Reserve a room at *Country Inn & Suites by Carlson*
- Score a few goals with a *Harrow Christian* wood hockey stick
- Grill a slab of ribs with *Famous Dave's BBQ Sauce*
- Go fishing in an aluminum boat from *Lund Boat Company*
- Experience the Rock Bottom Plunge rollercoaster at *Nickelodeon Universe, MOA*

Chapter Seven
Minnesota Memories

Nostalgic Notables
". . .You don't know what you've got till it's gone . . ."

- **Dayton's.** The 12-floor flagship department store in downtown Minneapolis had everything a shopper needed plus a few extras. Started in 1902 by George Dayton, the company developed and managed the first indoor malls starting with Southdale. Eventually Dayton's owned 64 locations in the region. Dayton's wasn't just a shopping destination. The Minneapolis store's eighth floor Christmas Display became a holiday tradition for many. After purchasing Marshall Field's the name changed for a short while until Macy's bought the department stores. Loyal customers still call Macy's "Dayton's," but it is not the same. At least Dayton's will forever be remembered with Mary Tyler Moore's famous hat toss from her TV series' opening credits.
- **Forum Cafeteria.** It was the most extraordinary cafeteria in the region. Converted from a movie house, it was synonymous with "good cheap eats in an Art Deco style" and right in the heart of downtown Minneapolis on Seventh Street. You could get full on fifty cents. The Forum was a favorite for 40 years.
- **Gambles Hardware** sold more than just a traditional hardware line. The originator of the chain store concept had its own house brand of appliances and bicycles. It even sold mini-motor scooters, called the "Doodle Bug." Started in

1920 by two friends, Bert Gamble and Phil Skogmo, as an auto dealership in Fergus Falls and then an auto supply store in St. Cloud that expanded into Gamble-Skogmo, Inc, with headquarters in St. Louis Park. An employee-owned conglomerate until 1947.

- **Kremer's Ben Franklin** was a variety store in Grand Rapids with a memorable lunch counter, great ten-cent chocolate malts, and hot dogs to die for. And everything else you might expect in a small town franchised five and dime. Furniture was on the upper level with a full hardware store in the basement. Kremer's put up quite a fight with the big box discount stores, but even its most loyal customers left to try America's new way of shopping. No more Kremer's.
- **Lincoln Del** was a true New York-style deli so it was always hard to get a table or booth. Lincoln Del South was in Bloomington. The West and East restaurants were located in St. Louis Park. Famous for its piping-hot, cheesy omelets, Delwich and corned-beef sandwiches, Lincoln Del reigned for 25 years. Rising real estate taxes and a multi-million dollar offer for the property, along the Bloomington freeway, by a car dealership persuaded the family to sell. If lucky, there will be a Lincoln Del in heaven.
- **Lyndale Hardware.** If Lyndale Hardware on 66th Street and Lyndale Avenue in Richfield did not have it, you did not need it. The free bag of hot popcorn was a long standing tradition. It has been years since it closed, but it's still missed. The owner loved the company but made more selling the land for a condominium development than the store could make in several lifetimes. The resulting 15-story building makes a fitting memorial.

- **Red Owl.** The neon Red Owl logo was like a bright spotlight beckoning for shoppers. The first Red Owl grocery store opened in 1922 in Rochester. Once a division of the failing Gamble-Skogmo Inc., by 1986 the wholesale grocer had expanded into six states with almost 500 stores thanks to franchising. The St. Louis Park store featured a Kiddie Corral with TV and children's books. Red Owl sponsored a movie night on Sundays on Channel 9 TV that received high ratings. The stores were in tip-top shape; the food was always fresh; and the carryout boys were extra friendly.
- **St. Paul Book & Stationery** stocked all the supplies and equipment you needed for home, office, or school. It was an upscale model for office stores and a great place to buy gifts. Teachers shopped there all the time. It served the Twin Cities well with its wonderful stores. If its demise was due to progress, something is wrong.
- **Sears on Lake Street.** In the beginning, there wasn't any place larger "west of the Mississippi." Sears Roebuck & Company retail store and catalog sales center in south Minneapolis was three blocks long and employed 2,000 people. The 16-story Art Deco style Sears Tower opened in 1928 and for 80 years was the place to shop. Rural shoppers liked the late Thursday and Saturday hours when it was open until 9 p.m. The hardware and sporting-goods sections were massive. It was a good place for family clothes, too. The catalog department was on the second floor. The counter was always three-deep in customers. At one time, the 11-acre site even had a Kroger grocery store. Sears closed its Lake Street store in 1994, and the historic building remained vacant until 2005 when the first phase a community driven renovation was completed. The multiple-use complex includes Allina

Hospitals & Clinics corporate headquarters; Midtown Exchange lofts, apartments and condominiums; and Midtown Global Market—an international themed food, restaurant, and arts and crafts market.

Minnesota Border Patrol? No wonder we have fewer illegals in the north. (Photo courtesy author's collection)

Soda Fountains
"What'll it be? Coke, malt, or Alka-Seltzer?"

> After I was married, I learned my wife, Mary, worked at the soda fountain in Whittemore Drug Store while she attended Grand Rapids High School. It was her first McJob. Her specialty was making banana splits. Whittemore's fountain was large with 20 counter stools. While we were visiting the soda fountain in the drugstore, by the Blandin Paper Mill, I mistakenly called her a "soda jerk." If you run into a former soda fountain server, refrain from the term, "soda jerk." They do not like it. It was a highly prized position. Maybe "soda jerker" would be more appropriate and respectful.
>
> — *Author's highlights*

Drugstores rank high on the list in American culture. They were a big part of growing up in Minnesota. Suddenly, drugstores were all over, not just on Main Street. Drugstores served the first carbonated beverages including *Coca-Cola*, syrup flavored *Coke* (usually cherry, lemon, or vanilla) and Phosphates (homemade soda pops mixed with one to five syrup flavors). Then they added ice cream and sandwiches (usually egg, chicken, or ham salad on white bread). Soda fountains were a nice profit center for the store. The smaller stores got by with as few as five stools. But 10 to 15 were more common. The majority of stores had just the plain-old-round seats. No backs. Many of the stools were not all that comfortable. Nevertheless, the owner knew what he or she was doing. Hard seats created faster turnover and better profits.

The servers were artists. They could dish up delicious sodas, sundaes, chocolate malts, and root beer floats in no time. The topping-off part, with gobs of whipped cream and a cherry on top, was always fun to watch. They also handed out *Alka-Seltzer* for quick heartburn or indigestion relief.

Bridgeman's first shop opened in Duluth in 1936. Bridgeman's expanded quickly throughout the state with 12 more parlors, plus one in LaCrosse, Wisconsin. One of their biggest ice cream parlors was in Minneapolis on Sixth and Hennepin. If the number of stools was the criteria for "best soda fountain," they won hands down, with more than 50. They also had lots of booths. Its original ice cream was delicious but high in butterfat content. Today they offer 24 flavors of healthier, but still premium ice cream and have franchises in five states.

Many of the F.W. Woolworth Company five and dime stores featured soda fountains (also called lunch counters). They were usually crowded, especially the Woolworth's on Nicollet and Seventh Street. When all seats were occupied, you would stand behind someone who looked like they were ready to leave. However, some could fool you by milking their second or third cup of coffee. Sometimes we did not practice "Minnesota nice."

Soda-fountain jobs soon went the way of elevator operators. They started disappearing in the early 1960s. Most were gone within 10 years. But it was no easy knockout. It took a combination of the increase and convenience of bottled soft drinks, commercially available ice cream and fast food restaurants to uproot them. As Mr. Johnson remarked after shutting down his fountain at Johnson's Drug Store in South Minneapolis, "apparently there is just not the need for soda fountains in today's scheme of living."

Movies—A Mini Vacation
Heaven was a double feature on Saturdays

> Kids never go to movies alone. You want someone along to share the experience. My best childhood cinema partner was Kenny, my three years older brother. He knew the part run, part walkway to downtown and all those big theaters. In 1939, we won free passes to the Minnesota Theater from *Collier's Weekly* magazine. The movie theater's lobby was bigger than anything we had seen. Ten ushers to take tickets, instead of the usual two. It blew me away! They were dressed to the nines in uniforms with gold buttons, braid and aiguillettes, white gloves, and shiny, black spit-polished shoes. I wanted to be one of them. Another thing new for us was Tommy Dorsey's 18-piece orchestra playing before the main feature. The Minnesota's stage and movie screen were huge, and they played organ music between the movies. Talk about getting your money's worth!
>
> — *Author's highlights*

At its peak in the 1940s, there was a movie house in nearly every neighborhood in Minneapolis. For only a dime, you could be entertained royally for two hours or more. Besides the neighborhood theaters Rialto, Avalon, and Franklin, you could go downtown to the bigger, plusher theaters: Aster, Orpheum, State, Pantages, Lyric, Grand (later Gopher), and Minnesota (later Radio City).

The **Aster Theatre** was a cinema treasure at Sixth and Hennepin in downtown Minneapolis. It may not have been the grandest theater, but it made up in character what it lacked in opulence. The Aster opened in 1916 with 900 seats, French countryside painted wall murals, and a large pipe organ. The Aster was famous for double features on Saturdays. You could see a Roy Rogers movie and a Charlie Chan movie, plus a serial that left you hanging. It was the only Minneapolis venue for Charlie Chaplin movies.

Seating an audience of over 4,000, the **Minnesota Theater** on Ninth Street South was the fifth-largest movie house in America when it opened its curtains in 1928. The building's exterior marquee height was eight-stories. The ornate French Renaissance styled interior lobby included huge marble columns three-stories tall, a crystal chandelier, and a marble staircase leading to the balcony. The velvet seat auditorium was so massive it was difficult finding the arched stage and silver screen if you sat in the balcony.

The **RKO Orpheum Theatre** on Hennepin Avenue premiered *Sister Kenny*, on July 22, 1946, at 8:30 p.m. That brought Hollywood stars and excitement to our city. *Sister Kenny* starred Rosalind Russell, Alexander Knox, and Dean Jagger. The film was based on Elizabeth Kenny's autobiography, *And They Shall Walk*. Kenny, an Australian, army-trained nurse discovered a treatment for polio and established The Sister Kenny Institute in Minneapolis in 1940. Minnesotans were proud to learn that the movie earned an Academy Award nomination for Miss Russell, who played Sister Elizabeth Kenny.

The Twin Cities was one of the motion picture industry's better markets. Theaters needed new movies, cartoons, newsreels, travelogues, and film shorts every week, and the major Hollywood studios tried to oblige. Columbia, MGM (Metro-Goldwyn-Mayer), Paramount Pictures, Republic, RKO (Radio-Keith-Orpheum), Selznick International Pictures, 20th-Century Fox, Universal, United Artists, and Warner Bros. could not produce features fast enough. There were lots of Republic's Roy Rogers and Columbia's Boston Blackie films, Mickey Mouse comedies, Fox Movietone News covering world events and shorts starring Robert Benchley, Edgar Kennedy, or Pete Smith. In addition, there were always movie trailers to entice you back.

Drive-in movie theaters became very popular for families from the late 1940s through the 1950s. The Twin Cities started with two, Roseville's *Rose Drive-In* and West St. Paul's, *Corral Drive-In* and increased to 80 throughout Minnesota including Duluth, Eveleth, Grand Rapids, International Falls, Pine City, Rice Lake, and Walker. The *Long Drive-In* (350 cars) in Long Prairie has been showing movies outdoors since 1956. The other remaining theaters include *Sky VU Drive-In* (180 cars) in Warren, *Cottage View Drive-In* (850 cars) in Cottage Grove, and *Vali Hi Drive-In* (800 cars) in Lake Elmo.

Go enjoy a night at the movies, indoors or outdoors. See the latest hit, with the hottest stars. There are always movie previews to bring you back again. Watch for films produced in Minnesota or starring Minnesota actors or former Minnesotans.

Minnesota may be known as the "Land of 10,000 Lakes," but we actually have 11,871 lakes. (All over ten acres in size.)

Chapter Eight
Prize Catches

Trivia Answers
Try quizzing your friends or family

- Where Judy Garland grew up:
  Grand Rapids. (The Garlands home is now a museum located south of the town on Highway 169.)
- American Cancer Society event held every November to encourage smokers to quit for a day:
  The Great American Smoke Out (Started by Lynn Smith, a Monticello newspaper editor, who called it "D" Day, for "Don't Smoke Day")
- Michael Langdon's TV show based on the books by Laura Ingalls Wilder:
  Little House on the Prairie
- Scandinavian delicacy that many Minnesotans love to hate during the holidays:
  Lutefisk (Served at Pearson's Edina Restaurant, featured on "The New York Times" front page for bravely cooking it.)
- America's largest indoor super-regional shopping mall:
  Mall of America in Bloomington (More than 500 stores, 50 restaurants, seven nightclubs, and 14 movie theaters with an amusement park landscaped in the heart of it. The major anchors are Nordstrom, Macy's, Bloomingdale's, and Sears.)
- Name of the ballpark where Ted Williams hit 43 homers:
  Nicollet Park (The eventual Baseball Hall of Famer played

for the Minneapolis Millers in 1938 at Lake Street and Nicollet Avenue in South Minneapolis.)
- America's first indoor shopping mall:
Southdale (Built in 1956 in Edina, Dayton's and Donaldson's were the two major anchors. It also featured a Red Owl Food Store.)
- Brand of breakfast food featured in America's very first singing commercial:
Wheaties (General Mills popular cereal ad aired on WCCO Radio 8-3-0 in 1926 and brought listeners a new kind of radio entertainment. Its selling message was put to music—"Have You Tried Wheaties?" The "jingle" started a revolution in the advertising industry.)
- Why the people in Blackduck are smarter than the people in New York City:
The people in Blackduck (population 748) know where New York City is (New Yorkers, population 8,143,019, don't know where Blackduck is.)
- Former phrase that many Easterners mistakenly hung on Minnesota:
Flyover Land (Shame on them! Those jealous people called Minnesota "flyover land" and implied that Minnesotans lived in a vast wasteland. However, when they came down to earth, they saw how wrong this myth was.)
- Rival border state in sports:
Iowa
Gopher vs. Hawkeye basketball and football games can get very heated. Local Twin Cities radio stations began telling "Iowa" jokes. Iowa fans reciprocated with a few of their own like these oldies:

Q. Why do Gopher football cheerleaders wear turtleneck sweaters?
A. To hide their flea collars.

Q. Why do Minnesotans go to bed so early?
A. So their candles won't burn out.

1st Iowan: Did you hear about that lazy Swede in Minnesota?

2nd Iowan: No. How lazy was he?

1st Iowan: He was so lazy he married a pregnant woman.

What did you do last summer? Bet the kids that write a paper about their visit to Ironworld, Chisholm, will earn a high mark. Its Iron Range Research Center is entertaining, educational, and open all year.

Minnesota Nice
No road rage in our neck of the woods

> My two grandsons, Brian and Justin Hill, asked recently while driving with me, why I gave a hand wave to the motorist behind my car. I explained that it was a simple acknowledgement to the driver for slowing down, to permit me space, when I came off the ramp. I do it all the time. It must be my "Minnesota nice" instinct working.
>
> God must have played a part in that tendency to just be nice and provided me and other Minnesotans with warm hearts and the ability to say thank you. Even former Minnesotans proudly display their "Minnesota nice" quality whether living in Arizona, California, Florida, or other warm communities. Like the old adage says: "You can take the person out of Minnesota, but you can't take Minnesota out of the person."
>
> *— Author's highlights*

Okay, once and for all, what is this **"Minnesota nice"** stuff all about? There seems to be a little confusion. Outsiders refer to the phrase in a derogatory way, but they are just jealous. What is wrong with being polite? **"Minnesota nice"** is a good thing. It is the ability to provide hospitality and courtesy to others. Statistics indicate Minnesotans file fewer civil lawsuits than residents do in other states. Now that is really nice.

Minnesota citizens are . . .

- voters, patriots, and quick to honor our military
- generous, renowned for volunteer work and donations
- recyclers and environmentalists

Minnesotans may be too good to be true . . .

- good neighbors, good hosts, and good people
- good sports, good stewards, and good Samaritans
- good cooks and good eaters
- good natured and good listeners
- good shoppers, good lookers, and good campers

Minnesotans can be . . .

- pioneers, achievers, and innovators
- collectors, joiners, and entertainers

Minnesotans are always on the go . . .

- easygoing
- churchgoing

Happiness in Minnesota is . . .

- rereading *Lake Wobegon* by Garrison Keillor
- exploring the Mississippi headwaters at Itasca State Park
- getting a nibble while fishing on Lake Minnetonka
- ice fishing in a carpeted fish house on Lake Mille Lacs
- deer hunting for 20 years
- watching the Vikings beat the Green Bay Packers
- shopping at the St. Louis Park Byerly's store

- visiting MOA
- teaching my grandson to drive
- receiving a tax refund
- being *Hooked on Minnesota*

A Minnesota sunset over Lake Edward at Shing Wako Resort, Merrifield, north of Brainerd. (Photo courtesy Shing Wako Resort)

10,000 Lakes

Our Land of 10,000 Lakes provide a world of recreation. (Photo courtesy Larry Young)

Mississippi Headwaters

From here at the Mississippi Headwaters, Lake Itasca, the Great River starts its 2,320 mile flow to the Gulf of Mexico. (Photo courtesy Visit Bemidji)

Minnesota's Great Wonders

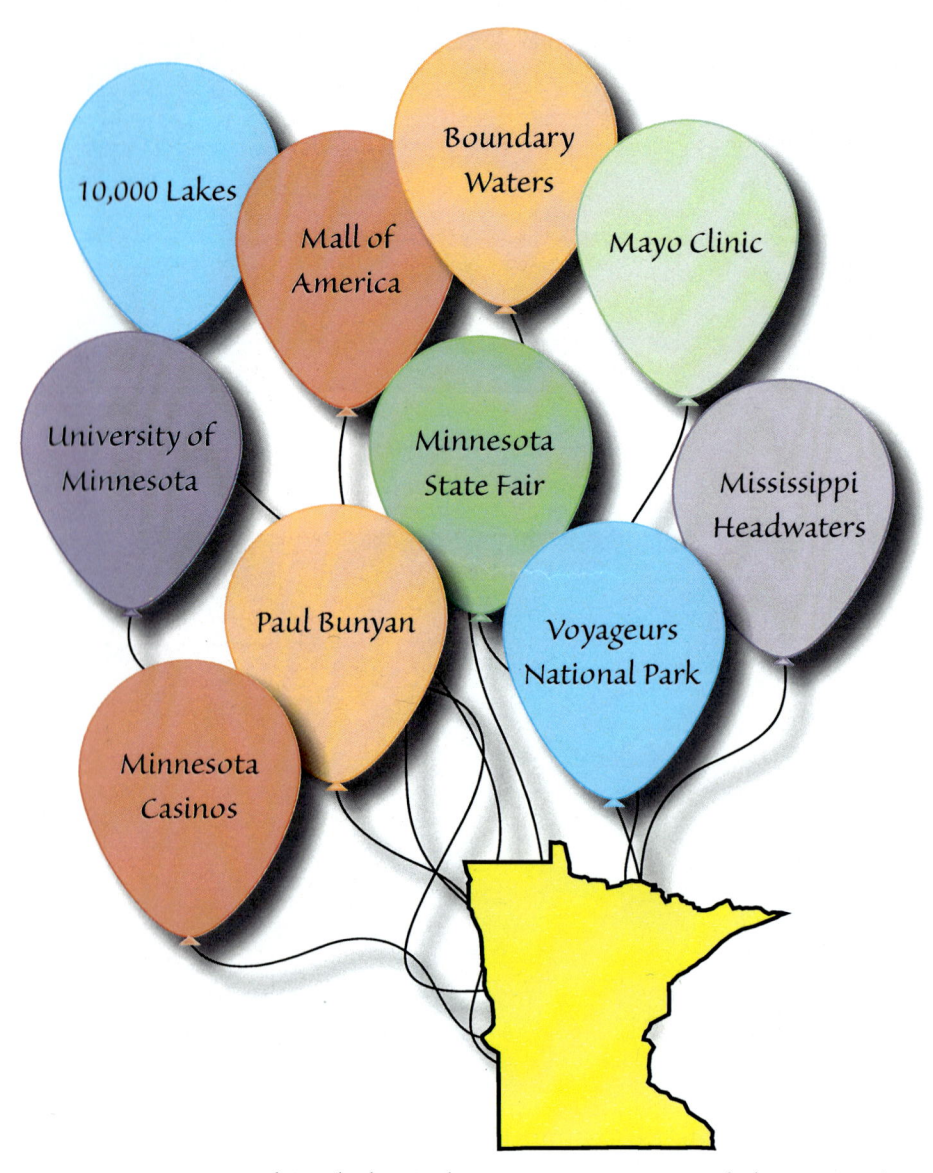

- 10,000 Lakes
- Mall of America
- Boundary Waters
- Mayo Clinic
- University of Minnesota
- Minnesota State Fair
- Mississippi Headwaters
- Paul Bunyan
- Voyageurs National Park
- Minnesota Casinos

Our Great Wonders help make Minnesota one of the nation's favorite places. Scattered throughout the state, many are natural; some manmade—all contributing to Minnesota's Good Life.

Boundary Waters

Canoeist surrounded by quiet wilderness at the Boundary Waters (BWCA) in northeastern Minnesota. (Photo courtesy Explore Minnesota Tourism)

Mall of America

MOA, Bloomington, offers a world of shopping and entertainment, including the first-ever, Nickelodeon Universe Theme Park, that Ashlee Simpson and friends helped open in March 2008. (Photo courtesy Mall of America)

Minnesota State Fair

The Minnesota State Fair is one of the world's largest, most visited expositions with an annual attendance over one million people. (Photo courtesy Minnesota State Fair)

Paul Bunyan

Paul Bunyan and Babe at home adjacent to the Bemidji Tourist Information Center since 1937. (Photo courtesy Visit Bemidji)

Minnesota Casinos

Minnesota has 18 casinos helping to make our state one of the nation's "fun centers."

Mayo Clinic

The Mayo Clinic, Rochester, has an international reputation and is considered the World's Health Clinic. (Photo courtesy Mayo Clinic)

University of Minnesota

A leader in education and cutting-edge research, The University of Minnesota is one of the most comprehensive public universities in the United States. (Photo courtesy University of Minnesota)

Voyageurs
National Park

Minnesota's Pot O' Gold—Voyageurs National Park—is found at the end of this rainbow over Lake Kabetogama. (Photo courtesy Alan Burchell)